The Father's Book

Because your family matters ...

Family matters is a brand new series from Wiley highlighting topics that are important to the everyday lives of family members. Each book tackles a common problem or difficult situation, such as teenage troubles, new babies or problems in relationships, and provides easily understood advice from authoritative professionals. The *Family Matters* series is designed to provide expert advice to ordinary people struggling with everyday problems and bridges the gap between the professional and client. Each book also offers invaluable help to practitioners as extensions to the advice they can give in sessions, and helps trainees to understand the issues clients face.

Titles in the series:

The Father's Book

Being a Good Dad in the 21st Century

David Cohen

JOHN WILEY & SONS, LTD

Chichester · New York · Weinheim · Brisbane · Singapore · Toronto

Published by   John Wiley & Sons Ltd
Baffins Lane, Chichester,
West Sussex, PO19 1UD, England

National   01243 779777
International   (+44) 1243 779777
e-mail (for orders and customer service enquiries):
cs-books@wiley.co.uk
Visit our Home Page on http://www.wiley.co.uk
or http://www.wiley.com

Other Wiley Editorial Offices

John Wiley & Sons, Inc., 605 Third Avenue,
New York, NY 10158-0012, USA

WILEY-VCH GmbH, Pappelallee 3,
D-69469 Weinheim, Germany

John Wiley & Sons Australia, Ltd, 33 Park Road, Milton,
Queensland 4064, Australia

John Wiley & Sons (Asia) Pte Ltd, 2 Clementi Loop #02-01,
Jin Xing Distripark, Singapore 129809

John Wiley & Sons (Canada) Ltd, 22 Worcester Road,
Rexdale, Ontario M9W 1L1, Canada

British Library Cataloguing in Publication Data
A catalogue record for this book is available from the British Library

ISBN 0-470-84133-8

Project management by Originator, Gt Yarmouth, Norfolk (typeset in 11.5/13 Imprint)
Printed and bound in Great Britain by Biddles Ltd, Guildford and King's Lynn
This book is printed on acid-free paper responsibly manufactured from sustainable
forestry, in which at least two trees are planted for each one used for paper production.

Contents

Contents

Contents

About the author

David Cohen is a psychologist, writer and film-maker. He has reported on mental health, immigration, why people make false confessions, sex, marketing to children, cults, finance, cigars and pirates for outlets as diverse as Channel 4, *Sunday Business*, Discovery, *Harper and Queens*, ITV and the *New Scientist*. Recent films include one on Grace Kelly for Channel 4 and *The Madness of Children*. He is currently working on a film on nuclear war games. His books include *Psychologists on Psychology*, *The Development of Play*, the best-selling *How to Succeed in Psychometric Tests* and *Fear, Greed and Panic*. He hopes one day to write a good poem.

He has two children and they, poor sods, were among the subjects for his PhD thesis on what makes children laugh. He now can't imagine what life would have been like if he hadn't had children.

To Alex and Katy,
Nicholas and Reuben
with love

Acknowledgements

As with all books, thanks are due to many. Julia Ross read part of the MS and made helpful comments. Lady Paddy Hunt drew my attention to Montaigne. Many thanks. David Hunt read the MS and made cracking wise points. Sam Boyce at Sheilland pushed me on. Dr Vivien Ward at John Wiley was the original begetter asking me to write on fathers. Helen Ilter put up gracefully with my being elusive during the production process. Neil Shuttlewood and his colleagues at Originator again did a marvellous job in producing my text.

Writing the book brought back many memories of being a young father and I'd never have been that if it hadn't been for Aileen La Tourette, the mother of my sons. Respect and love to her! Writing this also brought back memories of my parents, troubled souls both who, if there is an afterlife, are annoying the angels by complaining about each other.

The other debts are as personal – to Alex and Katy, Julia's children and to Nicholas and Reuben, my sons. Without them I'd have had less to write about. I still like being a father and a stepfather, and some thanks for that must be due to them.

I would also like to thank Michelle Ross-Stanton for digging out the United Nations and NSPCC statistics as efficiently as ever.

Introduction

In 2000, Tony Blair became the first man to become a father while Prime Minister for 200 years. A year later, the 70-year-old media tycoon Rupert Murdoch announced his third wife was pregnant. Since the 1980s, gender experts claim masculinity is 'in crisis'; the male psyche is wilting as social and sexual attitudes change too fast for the ballsy ones. Women insist on men who have great pecs and emotional intelligence too – the body of Brad Pitt and the soul of Sigmund Freud.

And the ballsy ones can't cope. The sperm count of the average male is falling, probably, doom mongers suggest, because we smoke too much, drink too much, stress too much and are exposed to 1,001 noxious chemicals.

Under this pressure, more and more men are opting out. According to the popular culture reflected in TV shows like *Sex in the City*, most of the best men are now gay, bisexual or opt for long periods of celibacy. In Sweden, the birth rate is so low the government has re-cruited Bjorn Borg to head an advertising campaign whose slogan is direct – Fuck for the Future. Failure to do so, will mean there soon won't be any Swedes.

In the rest of this book, in the interests of decency and in honour of (1) tennis and (2) *Star Trek*, the f-word will be replaced by the b-word. So, Swedes, I hope you will borg for your country's future ...

Despite all these post-modern *angsts*, sex still happens, relationships still happen, children still happen. In 1998, 129 million children were born according to the latest United Nations statistics. The United States saw 4.064 million births last year, the EC 4.1 million and Britain around 700,000. Swedes may disappear but the human race is safe.

Some men in 2000 will have had children by different women but, allowing for the occasionally sperm super hero who became a father twice, three times or more in the year, it's a reasonable guess that 120 million men became fathers in 2000 AD. I've never written a book with such a large potential readership.

I was 24 years old when Aileen had Nicholas, our oldest son, and I find it hard to remember what it was like not being a father. It was an event that changed my life more than any other. Before it happened, I was:

- frightened ... I couldn't cope ...;
- confused ... what become a father ... me ... no ... help;
- playing the familiar male game of I'm too incompetent to cope with squeamish aspects of biology. Moi, change a nappy? I have a degree from Oxford;
- stubborn and selfish ... being a dad was not going to stop me doing anything that I wanted to do.

Now I smile when I think back at how scared I was at the prospect of being a father. I would not have believed anyone who had told me, when Aileen was pregnant, that having children would be one of the great, sustaining, joys of my life.

I have no intention of painting too rosy a picture. As a father, you will be scared at times, embarrassed at times, mad at times, like when your partner doesn't want to make love in case the kids get bored with the telly and walk into your bedroom. Often, you'll be broke and sometimes in despair. Why can't you persuade your 10-year-old that being a human being does not require those £79 Nike trainers?

'But my mates will laugh at me, dad', he says.

'Don't care,' you say, reduced to the level of a 6-year-old brat.

'What if I get beaten up because it's the Nikes versus the non-Nikes in the playground. You don't understand, dad, it's war. It's only £79.'

You understand why I said 'despair'. Worse are the moments of panic. When Nicholas was born, for the first and only time in my life, I heard voices in my head. I was not in control. For about 15 minutes, while Nicholas was stuck in the birth canal, I prayed he would be safe and well. Inner voice replied. Yes, he would be safe but he would also be born speaking – and carrying an important message from God to Greenwich SE10. I'm a Jewish atheist by the way.

I managed to keep news of the divine message to Greenwich to myself, so I was not hauled off to the psychiatric ward.

Sixteen years later, Nicholas' birthday party ends up with at least three underage drinkers in vodka comas. But I don't hear voices this time.

Still, to the day I die, I will never forget the birth of either of my children. I will not forget the amazing experience of my 6-month-old son and I laughing at each other for hours. I will not forget how proud I felt when my other son, aged three, was given puzzles by the head teacher of a posh kindergarten. He looked seriously at her and said 'Ah, it's my exam.' She laughed; I laughed. 'I think he's just passed with flying colours,' she smiled.

And the panics don't stop. This morning my 22-year-old stepson, Alex, doubled with pain from an ulcer – yet again – and slumped down by the fridge. Ten minutes of terror till he was all right. And then the hassle of persuading him to get a doctor to examine him properly.

Never too young to leave home

I have wanted to write this book for nearly 20 years but when I suggested it to publishers in the early 1980s, they tended to dismiss the idea as absurd. We had seen the new lad book but the new dad book? No self-respecting bloke would be seen dead with such self-help junk – particularly not in Britain, HQ of the stiff upper lip where for centuries the UMU classes (upper middle and upper) had been sending their children off as young as possible to boarding school.

When our sons went as day boys to Dulwich College Preparatory School, the Headmaster, a superb old-style 'beak', Hugh Woodcock told us one parents' evening, he had an important announcement. A number of kindergarten parents had asked him if their offspring could be boarders. Mr Woodcock explained he was a fervent believer in boarding but even he thought 3- and 4-year olds were too young to be sent away from home!

Today, fathers are more involved with their children than ever before. Statistics show a steady rise in the number of men who attend the birth. In 1970, it was about 21%; in 1980, it was 42%. Some figures issued by the National Childbirth Trust claim that 96% of fathers in Britain attend the birth of their child. In perhaps 4% of families, the father is more responsible for childcare than the mother. Pressure groups like Gingerbread estimate that 500,000 fathers are looking after their children by themselves because of divorce, separation or death. Organisations like Fathers Direct and DIY Dads teach, train and argue passionately that 'fathers are important to their children and children important to their fathers. Involved fathers result in happier families.'

At the same time, sociologists like Laurie Taylor and his son Matthew point out the birth rate is falling not just in Sweden. People are asking 'just why should we have children?' for the first time. The narcissistic me culture, the proud gift of our recent past, has made many 20 and 30 somethings wonder if children are worth the hassle. Will being a parent mean less time for my tango classes? Might I have to devote too much energy to changing nappies and sterilising bottles which will make me too tired to get my diploma in web marketing?

I've had those thoughts. Maybe, if I hadn't become a father at 24, I would have made more memorable films, or written the novel I like to believe I always had in me . . . but I don't mind one bit.

What psychology teaches us about fathering

In *Reassessing Fatherhood* (1987), Charlie Lewis argued the 1970s saw a huge increase in research on fatherhood, partly in response to feminism. Yet despite Germaine Greer, Kate Millett, Sheila Rowbotham and many other passionate authors, people's lives had not changed dramatically by the mid 1980s. Looking after the children was still seen as women's work. A film I made in 1980, *When Men Become Mothers*, followed men who had been forced to be full-time fathers when their wives left them. The men were angry; their careers had suffered and they didn't know how to cope in a world that expected mothers to look after the children.

Lewis also looked at how much fathers cared for 1-year-olds. The details were depressing, especially as researchers suspect men often exaggerate what they really do. Lewis found that 62% of fathers said they never helped bathe the child, 53% never looked after the child on their own, 40% had never changed a nappy. Lewis quoted a 1979 study where one father admitted he could not change a nappy because 'I would vomit on the spot at the sight of the pooh.' He based this on his unhappy experiences mucking out a guinea pig cage.

I had not realised till then that Scots might be champion dads. In 1986, Malcolm Hill, a social work specialist in Glasgow, found that 40% of men sacrificed an evening or two a month to looking after the bairns so their wives could have a night out. It must be the kilts that lead to such true equality, true enlightenment.

As new parents, Aileen and I avidly read *Dr Spock's Baby and Child Care* which was already then in its 13th edition. Spock devoted about 10 pages out of 500 to the role of the father. Children did need fathers but it was no good the mother forcing her husband (in Spock's days it was all husbands) to spend time with babies and little children if they didn't want to. Better wait till junior was more like a real person before inflicting him, or her, on dad.

Even if fathers were keen, Spock told us, mother must not nag and make fatherhood interfere with important stuff such as doing your duties as a company man. In the evening, company man should try to spend an hour in 'rough-housing' play with the kids. But if work and the commute had left him too zonked to romp, dad shouldn't feel guilty. He should have his dinner, relax and veg out in front of the boob tube.

Spock really did live in a different universe. I can find no mention of child abuse in the 1970 edition of his book. I can also find no mention of what has become an issue in America – the way many men feel they were abandoned by their fathers as children. Anthony Astrachan in his book *How Men Feel* paints a dismal picture of the relationship between fathers and sons. One reason many men are diffident, ambivalent and often poor fathers is that their fathers did not teach them anything about being a father.

In *The Emperor's Embrace* (1999), the critic of psychoanalysis, Jeffrey Masson argues that humans have a lot to learn from species such as wolves, lions and, especially, emperor penguins. No beast apparently makes a more devoted dad than the emperor penguin who warms the egg on his feet for months, so protecting nipper penguin from the icy Antarctic gales. While warming the egg, dad also has nothing to eat and drink. This is heroic fatherhood indeed! Masson compares the experience of the infant penguin with that of the unfortunate writer Franz Kafka.

One of Kafka's works is a bitter letter to his father in which he complained that his father mocked him, bullied him and, certainly, did not love him. No penguin makes his kids suffer such trauma. On the other hand, if Kafka's dad had been an emperor penguin, we probably wouldn't have got Kafka's masterpiece, *The Trial*. Its hero, Joseph K is on trial for an offence he doesn't know; some critics argue the book has its roots in Kafka's unhappy relationship with his father. Undaddied, Kafka felt he had to prove himself worthy, worthy of being loved, worthy of just being alive.

Psychology should have studied fathers and fathering more than it has. One of the most famous concepts in psychology – Freud's Oedipus Complex – argues every male child unconsciously wants to kill his father and sleep with his mother. Psychoanalyst No. 2, Carl Jung, developed the ideas of the father archetype. The father archetype was all-wise, all-powerful and, of course, all-imaginary. And a major player in the unconscious, according to Jung.

Relatively few psychologists, however, have focused on research on fatherhood. The best known exceptions are Michael Lamb in America and Charles Lewis in Britain who has written a report for a number of charities called *What Good Are Dads?* (2001). Blendis (1988) also wrote an interesting PhD thesis on different types of fathers.

From 1945 until the 1980s, research on fatherhood concentrated on the so-called absent father. Children whose fathers had been away for long periods during the 1939–1945 war were less smart and less good. In the jargon, they had poorer academic performance and poorer emotional adjustment. It is a powerful image.

Today, black clergymen in Boston claim that 95% of the delinquents in that city have 'fatherlessness' at the root of their problems.

In Britain, at least, we have a paradox. Statistics show fathers have been more involved with their children in the last 10–15 years than ever before. So why is there more crime more mental health stress among children than ever before? A British government report out in 2001 claims that one child in five suffers from mental health problems.

There are a number of possible explanations for the paradox:

1   Fathers may be around more but the quality of time they spend with children is still poor.

2   Fathers are not really around much more. When psychologists survey them or video them 'interacting with children', the fathers play up to the camera. They exaggerate how much they do with their kids.

3   Fathers still make children feel they don't really care about them. They project indifference even when they are around. A father who is always down the pub or at the health club is unlikely to make his children feel good about themselves.

4   Changes in society encourage children to be assertive and some fathers do not cope with that well. The result is tension, and that stresses children out.

5   The expectations we have of children are changing. It is easier for children to feel failures than ever before. If you haven't got the Nikes, haven't got the exam results and haven't lost your virginity by the time you are 15, you're sad. Fathers are not good at helping children cope with these pressures.

There's also an academic oddity. Many of the most interesting writers on masculinity have approached the topic
from a gay perspective. And fatherhood is not a topic they
usually focus on. Historically, women have written more
on fathers than men. Ursula Owen, for example, has
looked at the relationships between fathers and daughters.
Academics, especially, don't usually write dispassionately
about fathers. My favourite fem-on-fathers text is by
two Dutch psychotherapists. *Unravelling the Father* includes a chapter titled 'Father is a money bag'. (I know
the feeling – an emptied out money bag).

The Dutch authors stress many fathers admit they
have 'negative qualities as a father' because they have 'a
lack of relational capacities, a lack of involvement'. Dutch
dad has no time, no personal skills and spends his life at
The Clog and Rembrandt.

Quoting Sylvia Plath's famous poem:

Daddy I have had to kill you
Daddy, Daddy, you bastard, I'm through.

Rosalind Miles in *The Children We Deserve* (1994) argues
most men, not just Kafka's dad, cannot fulfil the basic
requirement of parenting. Jealous sex-mad little boys
that we men are, we cannot give what Miles reckons is
most important, unconditional love. Children always
have to prove themselves to the 'old man'. Worse, the
old man sets up obstacles because unconsciously, he is
so jealous of the child for, once the child is born, the
'old man' will never be No. 1 again.

Miles is a distinguished and effective writer. But her
anger sometimes distorts her argument. Throughout this
book, she is a voice I argue with and I might as well start
the argument now. I am not sure what unconditional love
means. I think I know what loving children through thick

and thin involves – spending time with them, talking to them, never not returning their phone calls, giving reassurance, telling them they look great when they do and, sometimes, when they don't, endless practical as well as emotional support. James Watson, the son of a great psychologist, John B. Watson told me the best and closest times he had with his father were when they did woodwork together.

I am not suggesting doing woodwork is enough to show love, but it's exactly the kind of joint activity I talk about in this book as part of what makes good enough fathering.

Good enough fathering

Perhaps the most useful psychoanalytic ideas on parenting come from the late D. W. Winnicott (1896–1971).

Winnicott argued babies and children did fine as long as they had good enough mothering. He wrote relatively little about fathers, however, though he stressed the need for the father to give both mother and child emotional support. I have adapted some of his ideas to develop the concept of the **good enough father**. The good enough father is not perfect. But he tries, he is there and he does not commit the terrible sins – being abusive to children, denying emotional warmth, being indifferent.

One of the pleasures of writing a book is ferreting out long-forgotten sources. I have discovered a fiery 1930s book *Common Sense and the Child*. It had a preface by A. S. Neill who started the radical free school at Summerhill where children attend the classes they want to and have a real say in the running of the place. Every British government since the 1930s has tried to close Summerhill down at one time or another!

Neill was not an analyst himself but Freud's writings influenced his approach to education. Neill warned men against wanting their sons to be like them and he stressed the need for fathers to be aware of their faults. He wrote 'the man who sadistically gets an unconscious pleasure out of walloping his son's behind with a slipper will fail to benefit by the Chapter on sadism. His resistance ... will at once prompt him to dismiss the chapter as damned nonsense (and filthy stuff at that) and to bolster up his rationalised belief that a good whacking does a boy good.'

I hope readers will not be so blind to their own faults. In the pursuit of self-knowledge and to get men to think about how they feel about becoming or being fathers, I have included questionnaires at three places in the book. I have myself questioned the scientific validity of psychological questionnaires (see Shelley and Cohen, 1987). But my purpose here isn't scientific but to get men to analyse their feelings and to be honest with themselves.

The great German writer, Goethe (who was ironically one of Freud's heroes), famously said: 'If I knew myself, I'd run away.' Many women snipe men find it hard to be honest with themselves. Now be a real man and prove Goethe and many women wrong with a virtuoso display of honesty.

Box 1   A Few answers please

There are no right or wrong answers in this test, so it is genuinely not worth cheating.

1   Which of the following statements applies best to you? Do you think

(a)   I like routines   ☐

(b)   I enjoy new experiences   ☐

(c)   I have a tendency to panic   ☐

2   When you are faced with unusual events or things, which of the following is most likely to be your reaction?

(a)   I always cope

(b)   I get extremely anxious

(c)   I worry but I handle it usually quite well.

3   Which of the following best describes your relationship with your own father?

(a)   I know he loves me but he's never said

(b)   I have always tried to please him

(c)   He was cold and distant when I was upset

(d)   He's good fun and we love each other

(e)   None of the above. In which case write down your own description.

4   When was the first time you thought of being a father?

(a)   in your teens

(b)   in your 20s

(c)   you never thought about it till you were told it was going to happen

(d)   earlier than your teens.

5   In your present relationship is having a baby

    (a)   a joint decision

    (b)   your decision

    (c)   her decision?

6   Which of the following statements describes your feelings most accurately? 'When I discovered I was going to be a father, I was

    (a)   pleased

    (b)   pleased for her as she has wanted a child for a long time

    (c)   terrified

    (d)   I contacted my travel agent to book a 6 month holiday in Antarctica'.

There need not be just one answer to the question that follows.

7   Which of the following statements best describes your attitude? 'When I discovered I was going to be a father, I was

    (a)   scared I would not be able to afford it

    (b)   scared that it meant the end of my youth

    (c)   scared by the responsibility

    (d)   scared my mum would keep moaning I had no idea how to be a father*

    (e)   scared it would interfere with my career*'

(*for example, if you could be frightened of the impact on your career and about your mum, tick both d and e).

8 Who was the first person you told you were going to be a father?

   (a)   your other children

   (b)   your parents

   (c)   your ex-wife

   (d)   your current wife who ... didn't know there was another woman in your life

   (e)   your lawyer.

The following question is just for those who already have children.

9 Write down five things you like about being a father if you have a child or children.

_____

_____

_____

_____

_____

The following question is just for prospective fathers.

10 Write down up to five things you don't like about having children

_____
_____
_____
_____
_____

11 If you are not yet a father, write down five things you are looking forward to about having children.

_____
_____
_____
_____
_____

12 For prospective fathers, write down up to five things that make you anxious if you were to have children.

_____
_____
_____
_____
_____

13 Which of the following statements is nearest the truth for you? 'Now that I'm going to be a father

(a)   I expect my life will change totally

(b)   I expect my life will change and it worries me

(c)   I have no intention of letting some baby change my life'.

14 Which of the following statements are true about your relationship with your own father?

    (a)   my own father is – or was – easy to talk to

    (b)   my father was often not around when I was a child

    (c)   my father is – or was – always very distant with me.

15 If I am confronted with a dirty nappy, the following is what I do or think I will do

    (a)   say to the mother it needs to be changed

    (b)   ring my mother

    (c)   do it myself

    (d)   summon the butler

    (e)   say I'm sorry I know it's wrong but I just can't face it.

16 Which of the following statements expresses your attitudes best?

    (a)   I hope my children will learn not to make the same mistakes that I have made

    (b)   I hope my children will realise I know more about life than they do

    (c)   I get very anxious about my children.

17 You have just shouted at your 5-year-old daughter. Which of the following is your most likely response?

(a)   you do nothing – you feel she deserved it –
      that's it

(b)   hope that you did not frighten her too
      much

(c)   check to see how she is feeling

(d)   check to see how she is feeling and if she
      understands why you had to shout at her.

18 Your child refuses to eat her/his fish and chips.
Do you tell her?

(a)   I'd like to know why – you always liked
      fish and chips

(b)   you're lucky to have any food when so
      many children in the world are starving

(c)   worry she is developing finicky eating
      patterns which can lead to eating
      disorders

(d)   you're not getting any sweets till you
      finish your food.

19 You hate swimming but your 8-year-old wants
you to take him/her to the pool. Do you?

(a)   stop whatever you're doing and take him
      or her

(b)   say you're tired now but you will go
      swimming soon

(c)   point out you've got better things to do

(d)   tell the child to shut up and stop
      bothering you.

20 Next door comes to complain that your child
has been throwing stones at their cat. Do you?

   (a)   tell the neighbour to borg off

   (b)   tell your child to stop doing it – being cruel to animals is wrong

   (c)   smack your child to teach them what the cat feels like

21 Which of the following statements is closest to your own views about child welfare?

   (a)   I'm not surprised some children get abused – they ask for it

   (b)   I know children can drive you mad but that's no excuse for hitting them

   (c)   People who are sick enough to abuse children should be thrown in jail for ever

   (d)   children need to be protected but somehow you have to let them run some risks or they'll never really be able to take care of themselves.

22 Sometimes, I have to cook for my children. When I do

   (a)   I worry about whether they are getting the right diet

   (b)   I resent having to do it – it's their mother's job

   (c)   always find it's really fun.

The answers to the quiz are on p. 24.

Other tests are to be found later in the book. The answers are at the end of this chapter.

By the time you have done the other two question- naires you should have a good sense of your own views about being a father, and what aspects of fatherhood make you both happy and anxious.

In the chapters that follow, I use research, reportage and personal experience to give an up-to-date account of the art, science and human condition of being a father. I try to give advice in some areas without being too preachy and I also suggest games fathers can play, since we are often a little inhibited. One can't do that without some humour. The practical advice is the hardest.

Chapter 1, 'A history of fathers', starts with the Bib- lical story of Abraham and Isaac, a tale many psychoana- lysts think is powerful as it expresses the ambivalence in the father–son relationship. Today, when there are so many concerns about child abuse, we can't help seeing being schlepped to the top of a hill to be sacrificed to the Lord as a fairly extreme form of abuse. The chapter also looks at how social attitudes about fathering have changed dramatically over the last 400 years.

Chapter 2, 'Becoming a dad', covers the time from when you learn you are becoming a father to just after the birth. It examines the anxieties men feel, the experi- ence of being present when your child is born, prepara- tions for the birth and the feelings – good and bad – which becoming a father can trigger. This chapter also looks at what needs to happen for babies and parents to bond. I also explore attachment theory, the surprising skills of the newborn and work which claims you can tell your child's basic personality by 4 months of age.

Chapter 3 is called 'The growing mind'. To be a good enough father, it helps to know something about child development. I examine the work of the eminent Swiss psychologist, Jean Piaget, at children's memory, at recent

The intant philosopher

work which suggests children today have a higher IQ than children did 50 years ago and what the implications are for fathers.

Chapter 4 is called 'Pretending, play and lying'. Since 1890, psychologists have tried to define the purpose of play. Play allows children to practice various skills and roles and, through that, children realise that other people have other ideas and feelings. Fathers sometimes don't find it easy to play, to get down on the floor and pretend to be an elephant. Social inhibition, stress and that very important psychological motive 'I'll just look too silly if I do that' paralyses some men. Learn how to play with your children, how to cope with their lying – if they pretend, they lie – and to grow in the process. I also look at the latest research on autism which some link to the inability to pretend.

Chapter 5, 'Do as I say', examines rules and discipline. Both parents have to deal with discipline but, in the past, the great threat was, 'I'll tell your father'. That is no longer so much the case, but fathers are still crucial in matters of discipline. Research makes it clear what the most effective techniques of discipline are, yet millions of parents refuse to listen. Why?

Chapter 6, 'A mind to school', covers what fathers can, and can't, do to help their children to learn. Parents have an important part to play in teaching their children key skills such as reading. But this can be a difficult area for two reasons. First, some parents can be too pushy. Second, as children get older, they may become lazy and try to persuade dad not just to help with their homework, but to do it all for them. I also look at attention-deficit disorder.

Psychologists and biologists have debated for over a century whether heredity and environment, nature and nurture, are more important. Everything suggests there is no such battle. Nature and nurture work together. Children are biologically wired to be born into a social environment which should help them adapt and grow.

Chapter 7, 'Heartache', deals with how to handle serious psychological and health problems including depression, attempted suicide, anorexia and the guilt that parents often feel if any of those happen.

Chapter 8, 'You're not my real dad', examines divorce, stepfamilies and socks. These are, of course, different but they are linked. There are over 3 million stepfamilies in Britain; only 41% of children live in traditional families with their biological parents. It's not easy to be a good father when you only see your child once a week or even less, when you only see your child at an access centre. It is also not easy to be a good father to someone else's children. What help does research offer teaching us to cope? Finally, the social significance of socks will be revealed. But only right at the very end . . .

Chapter 9, 'Relationships carry on', examines the pressure babies and young children create on relationships. Most couples expect that having a child will make them happier, will be the icing on the cake. True, sometimes, but having a child is, according to stress indexes, as stressful as having to cope with a death.

Chapter 10, calculates 'The price of being a dad'. The cost is getting higher every year partly because children today are more exposed to marketing than ever before and very conscious of brands. I also look at the tangled questions of pester power and phone and Internet bills. Woody Allen wrote a piece for the New Yorker about a famous philosopher's laundry list. I go one better and on p. 241 I reproduce part of our phone bill. Analysis of this terrifying document will provide real insight into the battle of the generations and suggest tactics on what to do if your 14-year-old (who understands better than you how to program a computer) is accessing softporn sites through the web. It's a moral issue, sure, but Porno-Phone also costs 50p a minute.

Chapter 11 quakes before 'Teenage traumas'. Teenagers are a relatively recent phenomenon. They don't seem to have existed before the 1950s when James Dean catapulted them into being. Then came the mods, the skins, the rockers, the flower children, the punks, the deadheads. For a father, it's again a fine line between letting them get away with murder and being too heavy handed. How do you help children become individuals and individuals who will challenge you? This chapter also deals with sex. I get personal too. My own teenage experiences were strange. My parents left me in a flat in the West End just before my 13th birthday. My school never found out I was living on my own.

Chapter 12 looks at 'Replicas and the dependency paradox'. While children grow up quicker than ever before, we are also seeing more and more dependence from teenagers and 'children' in their 20s and even 30s. In Britain the cost of housing and in America the cost of education make it hard for teenagers and young people to leave home and live independently. That dependency exposes fathers to a temptation, to want their children to be like them.

But none of the problems should put you off one of the greatest of all human adventures.

Being a good father today is about love, care, providing for, and then letting your children go, so that you can have a good relationship with them for the rest of your life.

I hope to be alive in my 80s, even 90s, when my sons will be in their 50s and 60s. I hope I will die before them because I can think of nothing more cruel than having to bury one's child. This book is mainly about being a father of young children but it's worth pausing to think. Your relationship with your children will probably be one of the longest of your life.

Heavy stuff. And if you focus on the heavy stuff, you'll get too anxious and feel far to prone to guilt. So stick the previous sentimental-serious paragraph somewhere at the back of your mind and get on with the interminably practical business of being a good dad in the here and now.

Answers to quiz on p. 12

The point of this test is not to make you feel good or bad but to help you understand yourself more. Answers to open-ended questions should be specially useful in giving you insight into your own personal quirks (are you warm, W; anxious, A; closed, C; or stable, S?):

1 a. *S*   b. *W*   c. *A*

2 a. *C*   b. *A*   c. *S*

3 a. *C*   b. *A*   c. *C*   d. *W*
   e. see what you've written and look below

4 the only score that matters is c for which you get 2
C's

5 a. *S*   b. *W*   c. *C*

6 a. *W*   b. *W*   c. *A*   d. *C*

7 you score 1 *A* for every one you tick

8 a. *W*   b. *W*   c. *C*   d. *C*   e. *C*

9 Again see what you've written and look below

13 a. *S*   b. *A*   c. *C*

14 a. *W*   b. *A*   c. *C*

15 a. *C*   b. *P*   c. *S*   d. *P*   e. *A*

16 a. *S*   b. *C*   c. *A*

17 a. *C*   b. *A*   c. *S*   d. *S*

18 a. *S*   b. *C*   c. *A*   d. *C*

19 a. *W*   b. *S*   c. *C*   d. *C*

20 a. *C*   b. *S*   c. *C*

21 a. *C*   b. *W*   c. *C*   d. *S*

22 a. *A*   b. *C*   c. *W*

These questions are designed to see how people score on
the following attitudes:

- Warm v Cold
- Closed/Punitive v Liberal/Open
- Anxious v Free
- Stable v Neurotic

(See below for answers to the four open-ended questions.)

First add up the number of **W**s for Warm, **A**s for Anxious, **C**s for Closed, **S**s for Stable that you have scored:

- maximum score of **A**s for Anxious is 16;
- maximum score of **C**s for Closed is 16;
- maximum score of **S**s for Stable is 11;
- maximum score of **W**s for Warm is 9;
- the **P** score is irrelevant but you are pathetic over nappies!

You must also be honest in the way you interpret your answers to the open-ended questions.

- If you score more than 8 **A**s, you tend to be anxious about being or becoming a father.
- If you score under 2 **C**s, you are too relaxed about it.
- If you score over 8 **C**s, you have a tendency to be closed and punitive which will almost certainly stem from your own childhood experience.
- If you score under 3 **C**s, you are probably frightened of admitting some aspects of being a father which trigger deep anxieties that you get defensive about – and therefore don't admit even to yourself. We all have closed parts of our personality.
- If you score over 6 **S**s, you are pretty sensible and realistic about fatherhood and its problems.
- If you score less than 2 **S**s, you are unrealistic about it.
- If you score more than 5 **W**s, your basic tendency is warm, open and enthusiastic about fatherhood. Under 2 **W**s, then worry.

Look now at the open-ended answers. Did you find it easy to list five good things about being a dad? Did you want to add more? Or was it the bad things you found easy to list? Talk the results over with the woman in your life. If you score high on Closed, think about whether this is the parenting style you want to have. There are no right or wrong answers. But we are not helpless and we are responsible. If you want to change, you can at least try. Many fathers don't realise how anxious and how angry they can get and the effect on their families.

1

A history of fathers

Just before his 80th birthday, Prince Philip made headlines by allegedly letting friends tell his biographer Graham Turner that he believed his son would not make an effective king. Prince Philip had to take the apparently unusual step of both writing to, and telephoning, his eldest son to say sorry. And that's the truth, according to the tabloids.

The Windsor rows are dynastic small beer compared to those of the Nepali royal family. On 1 June 2001, Prince Dipendra was serving drinks to his family when he made his excuses and left. He returned a few minutes later in combat fatigues, brandishing a machine gun. In the next 15 minutes, he killed his father and nine other members of the royal family. One account claims the last thing his father said to Prince Dipendra was that he should come back properly dressed. You don't have cocktails in combat gear.

Rivalry between fathers and sons is as old as family life. According to Freud, its roots are prehistoric. In his

weird *Totem and Taboo*, Freud argued the primal drama
was a conspiracy of sons against their fathers. Wanting to
possess the women in the tribe, the sons murdered their
father. Then the band of brothers felt so guilty, they set
the dead father up as a totem. Safely dead, Pop could be
worshipped. Then, things were never simple with Freud,
the guilty sons had to punish themselves. So the lads
established the taboo against sleeping with their mother.
In their perfect guilt, they devised a brilliant penance.
And the poor schmuks had no Neanderthal Freud to
listen to them on a Stone Age couch.

Totem and Taboo is a wonderful fable and it merits
scholarly consideration. So does the history of fathers.
In a short book, all I can offer are illustrations which
show being a good father has meant different things at
different times and in different cultures. It's important
to remember that because so many of us carry images in
our heads of what being the perfect dad will be like.

Woody Allen versus history

The artist who has done best out of Freud is, of course,
Woody Allen. Years of analysis do not seem, however, to
have fine-tuned his parenting skills. When Woody Allen
fought for the custody of his adopted son Moses, the judge
summed up the great film-maker's performance as a
parent critically. The judge said:

> *He did not bathe his children. He did not dress them
> except from time to time and then only to help them
> put on their socks and jackets ... He does not know
> the name of Moses' teachers or about his academic*

*performance. He does not know the name of his chil-
dren's dentist. He does not know the name of his
children's friends.*

A good Victorian father would have been astonished by
the notion that he should bathe his son. And if Woody
Allen had been a father in Biblical Israel, he could have
argued he was almost a perfect father. Maybe he wasn't
hot on the bathing but did he strap his son to a donkey and
take him to the top of a mountain to murder him?

Sacrificing the son

The story of Abraham and his beloved son is one of the
most dramatic in Genesis. The Lord told Abraham to take
Isaac to the top of the Mount Moriah with a knife and a
kettle. The Lord promised to consecrate Abraham as a
high priest, a ceremony that needs a sacrifice. 'And your
beloved son Isaac shall be the sacrifice', added the All-
merciful.

Did Abraham tell the Lord not to be absurd, not to
break one of his own soon-to-be-published Ten Com-
mandments 'Thou Shalt Not Kill', or just sorry, God,
family comes first.

I should coco. Abraham did as he was told.

When Isaac asked why they were not also bringing a
lamb with them, Abraham didn't tell his son the truth.
The Lord would provide the sacrifice. Abraham failed to
mention how personally involved Isaac was since he was
for the chop himself.

As we all know, it was all a test and a tease. When they
got to the top of the mountain, God had thoughtfully

arranged for a ram to have its horns caught in a thicket. So the ram copped it and Isaac did not end up as pot roast.

Genesis is vague on whether Isaac realised his father had been ready to kill him for the Lord. It does not explore what effect the drama had on their future relationship. I get into trouble if I tell my son he shouldn't smoke so much. As it happens, sacrifice of the first-born son was common in the ancient world. Neighbours of Abraham, such as the Moabite King Meshga, and the Ammonite kings often did away with their sons to appease their gods.

Greek myths also don't show fathers at their best. Mega-god, Kronos, father of Zeus, ate his own children without even cooking them first. Another myth tells the story of Phrixus. His father King Atahamas had two wives and, when famine hit his kingdom, he consulted the priestess of Apollo. She gave the inevitable advice. Keep the gods happy, have a juicy sacrifice. Like Abraham, the King was ready to send his son for the mountain top chop.

Again, though, there was a happy ending. Zeus, chief of the gods, old greybeard and tousle locks, sent a messenger who announced piously:

Zeus does not like human sacrifices
So, yet again, the child was spared.

It doesn't take supreme insight to see myths and Genesis point to tension in the father–son relationship. The ambivalence has some simple causes. Fathers love their sons and want to protect them but fathers are also jealous; they see their sons who are strong, beautiful and have their lives before them. Meanwhile, the fathers are getting closer to the grave every moment. One way to cope with these ambivalences is for the father to teach the son and, especially, to teach the son to be like him. For 5,000 years, fathers have passed their skills so their sons can be farmers, soldiers, accountants, dentists and doctors. When a father smiles 'I am so proud of my son, he is just like me,' remember, dad is praising himself.

I've picked a number of quotes which reflect both that wisdom and that ambivalence.

Children begin by loving their parents. After a time, they judge them. Rarely, if ever, they forgive them.
Oscar Wilde

When one has not had a good father, one must create one.
Nietzsche

It is with great pleasure that I see the preservation of children has become the Care of Men of Sense. In my opinion this Business has been left too fatally long to the management of women who cannot be supposed to have a proper knowledge to fit them for the task, notwithstanding they look upon it as their own province.
William Cadogan 1764 in his *Essay on Nursing.*

The words a father speaks to his children in the privacy of the home are not overheard at the time but, as in a whispering gallery, they will be clearly heard at the end and by posterity.
Richter

When a father gives to his son, both laugh; when a son gives to his father, both cry.
Yiddish proverb

One must have the courage to give children up; their wisdom is not ours.
Chardonne

The principal determinant of modern neurosis is the personality of the father which is always lacking in some way or another, whether absent, or humiliated divided, or sham.
Jacques Lacan, psychoanalyst

Through the course of history, infinitely more children were killed by their parents than parents killed by their children.
George Devereux

Whipping will work but an imperfect cure ... frequent beating is therefore to be avoided.
Michel de Montaigne

It is frustration at the breast and crucially weaning that makes the infant turn to the father's penis and become aware of the triangular situation.
Hanna Segal writing about the Oedipus Complex – the triangular situation as seen by the psychoanalyst Melanie Klein

Very often we are more moved by our children's frocklings, games and infantile nonsense than by their mature acts. It is as if we loved them for our amusement, as monkeys, not as human beings.
Michel de Montaigne

How many children do you have?
No children.
No children – what do you for aggravation?
Yiddish proverb

It's not surprising, of course, that we think deeply about the father–child relationship because it is at the root of our identity.

Honour thy father but don't expect too much from the old man

In 1580, Michel de Montaigne wrote a strikingly modern essay on the affection of fathers for their children. Montaigne felt he had an idyllic childhood. 'I was only whipped twice' and 'I felt I owed the same upbringing to my children'. All of his children died 'at nurse', however, apart from his daughter Leonora, so he could never put his ideas into practice.

Montaigne pointed out many fathers were stingy to their children once they had grown up. He felt 'it is unjust that an old broken down half dead father should, alone in his chimney corner, enjoy wealth' while his offspring were so poor they were sometimes driven to stealing. He catalogued many cases of young French aristocrats who took to thieving because their dads left them so broke. The old men were jealous, and jealousy led to bitterness. Often, children couldn't wait for their father to die so that they could inherit, Montaigne wrote. The fathers were also psychologically mean.

Montaigne said: 'It is wrong to deprive the young of familiarity with their fathers in the hope of keeping them in awe and obedience. This is the most futile farce.' Fathers should rejoice in their children apart from those who turned out to be savage monsters.

When sons died in battle, fathers were sometimes inconsolable, not only because of the death but because of what they had failed to do for their sons. The Maréchal de Monluc was a friend of Montaigne. Monluc's son was 'a truly brave gentlemen' who died on the island of Madeira. But the son never knew what his father really felt for him. Monluc spoke to Montaigne of 'his sorrow and he stressed among his many regrets, the heart breaking grief he felt at never having opened his heart to the boy. He had always put on a stern face, the grave father and so he had lost the chance to know and appreciate his son ... He had lost the chance to tell his son the love he had for him and the high opinion he had of his abilities.'

'That poor boy only saw me as a grim man with a grim frown and he's died thinking I could neither love him nor value him,' Monluc said. He had let his son only see 'a foolish mask' and was afraid that his son's feelings towards him 'must have been cool since all I ever show-ed him was gruffness and my behaviour was often tyran-nical.' There was little Montaigne could do to console his friend except warn other fathers not to behave like that.

The involved father

The historian Linda Pollock, in her study of diaries, found a surprising number of fathers from the 16th century who were interested in how their children developed. Often the father was present when the child did something of note. Moore (1779–1852), for example, described how his 10-month-old daughter learned to walk. He wrote:

> Our little Barbara is growing very amusing. She started yesterday in walking; that is, got up off the ground by herself, and walked to a great distance without anyone near her. Bessay [the mother] was almost flying out of her mouth all the while with fright but I held her away, and would not let her assist the young adventurer.

But many Victorian fathers had a much more rigid attitude especially to their sons. The philosopher James Mill made sure his son could read by the age of 3. By the age of 12, J. S. Mill had been introduced to Shakespeare, Plato, the historian Gibbon and the philosophical works of David Hume. Mill took his son walking but these expeditions were educational. Father and son admired nature and discussed the meaning of meaning. In his autobiography, J. S. Mill said he never had time for play as 'no holidays were allowed lest the habit of work be broken.'

Mill does not seem to have hated his father, however. He did become a solitary and bookish young man. The reason why he felt no resentment may be that, while he had a pushy father, J. S. Mill did not feel neglected. His father paid him a great deal of attention and was hardly indifferent.

The older Mill seems to have been the very model of an insufferable Victorian father. Father was head of the family, fount of all knowledge and discipline. Rosalind Miles cites an 1844 poem as proof of what she sees as such typical male arrogance:

The father gives his kind command
The mother joins, approves
The children all attentive stand
Then, each obedient moves.

The Victorian father's authority was partly rooted in religious faith. By the end of the 19th century, however, the new-fangled science of psychology offered often insecure mothers and fathers answers to how to bring up their children. And the advice was now based on evidence or, at least, experiments.

Fathers know best ...
the behaviourist father

One of the first scientific experts on parenting was John B.
Watson (1878–1958), the founder of the psychological
school known as behaviourism. Watson's father Pickens
had run away when his son was young. When John B. had
become rich and famous, Pickens turned up at his New
York office in search of a handout. With a father like that,
Watson was always sceptical about how loving parents
were.

Watson wrote an influential book with his second wife,
Rosalie Rayner. *The Psychological Care of the Infant and
Child* (1929) argued fathers had an important role to play
and one special contribution to make. Mothers were likely
to be too sentimental; they kept on smothering baby with
hugs and kisses. Most mothers, Watson barked, should be
indicted for 'psychological murder ... I know hundreds
who want to possess their children's souls.' Fathers had to
protect babies from smother love but, unfortunately, were
more obsessed with obedience. 'Most fathers should be
punished for the idiotic parental duty dogma they try to
instil in their young.' The dogma was that children owed
their parents. 'Children don't owe their parents anything,'
Watson said. Especially not handouts 30 years after dad
walked out.

Watson outraged women's groups complaining 'kissing the baby to death is just about as popular a sport as
it has ever been'. Ever the methodical scientist, Watson
and his wife had gone on a 3-hour drive with friends
and noticed the mother kissed the baby 32 times.
Watson shocked the Mothers Union even more by suggesting that all this kissing 'is at bottom a sex seeking
response.'

Watson's son James told me he thought his father was influenced by Freud. A child who was touched too much by his mother might fall in love with her and Freud did link that with homosexuality. His father kept his physical distance very deliberately, James recalled, and it did not make his son happy. 'I respected my father as a man but not as a father really,' the younger Watson told me. When Rosalie died at the age of 37, James felt the lack of affection at home terribly. His elder brother rebelled. He became a psychoanalyst totally opposed to his father's ideas and eventually committed suicide.

Nevertheless, John B. Watson was an active father. He taught his sons woodwork every weekend and he believed that mother, father and children should regularly sit down to discuss what we would now call 'issues'. Children could talk about difficult matters sensibly. Parents could explain reasonably why a child should be polite and should not masturbate – especially not in front of his aunts. Watson's ideal was the kindly, rational but cool father.

As a father, Watson was unusual then in spending so much time with his children. Looking at parenting between 1900 and 1950, Humphries and Gordon (1989) report interviews with very few men. Magazines like *Good Housekeeping* and *Woman and Home* offered mothers endless advice on how to bring up their children. But neither they nor any other publication had much to say to fathers. Few men seemed to want to be less marginal. Few absentee fathers felt they missed anything, Humphries and Gordon record.

Fiction supports that indifference. In George Orwell's novel about 1930s England, *Coming up for Air*, the hero George Bowling is always irritated by his children. They make too much noise, they keep on wanting money for sweets and comics. Before the 1980s, when fathers did have to take on childcare, it was almost always because of economic disaster. They were unemployed or disabled.

The woman had to become the breadwinner. In Lanca-
shire, unemployed men who had to stay at home and mind
the kids were sneeringly called 'Mary Annes' – almost
nancy boys even though they were dads.

The useless-at-parties syndrome

A nice insight comes from the mid-20th century. In 1952,
The Times published one of its light fourth leaders. The
Carriage Waits outlined the predicament of a father who
had to fetch his children back from a party, 'some fathers
volunteer, some – perhaps less rarely – are detailed for this
duty.' The father first had to know just where 'Ursula's
party is taking place before setting out on his errand of
mercy.' Once he finds the party, father faces 'the contin-
uous din of tin whistles, mouth organs and hooters punc-
tuated by the bursting of balloons, each explosion being
followed by a wail of grief of rage.' All too too hard for the
poor man.

   While Ursula's mother fetches the children's coats,
'the man finds himself becalmed in a group of ladies ...
and feels at a disadvantage. The only possible topic of
conversation is obviously children and these ladies know
so much more than he does about (so to speak) the points
of a child.' And so the father finally leaves – Ursula will
tell him who his children are in case he does not recognise
them – and he feels a total failure, as he has made 'heavy
weather' of what ought to be simple.

   The Times did not speculate on the impact father's
obvious inadequacy would have on his children and especially on his little boys. Did the boys learn the unspoken
lesson that a male can hardly be expected to cope with the
most basic childcare?

In Britain, two other factors have helped shape our ideas of fatherhood over the last 50 years. First, it has been considered acceptable for the social elite to send its children – and especially its sons – away to boarding school. Generations of men spent their childhood away from home and away from their father. The adult male they related to most was often the house master who was, of course, as much a father to the other fifty or a hundred boys in his house.

Second, Britain's royal family does not seem to have had any spectacularly successful father–son relationships. Edward VIII was regarded by his father George V as something of a wastrel. George VI had no sons. Prince Philip is apparently critical of Prince Charles. After the massacre in Nepal, a cartoon in the *Evening Standard* showed the Queen and Prince Philip wandering around Buckingham Palace in bullet proof vests ... just in case Prince Charles got any ideas! *Private Eye* carried a similar story in which Charles dreamed of imitating the actions of his pal in Nepal.

In the social elite in other countries, the assumptions about fathers and sons can be very different, though.

Cross-cultural

I don't think there are obvious parallels between Britain and Korea, and it's in Korea that I came across one of the most touching declarations from a father to a son. In 1980, the Korean winner of the 2000 Nobel Peace Prize, Kim Dae Jung, wrote a letter to his son from prison. Kim was jailed by the South Korean military dictatorship on many occasions up to 1986 as he fought for democracy.

Kim spoke of the pleasure his son had given him when 'you were riding beside me.' He also wrote:

I feel a heavy weight as I think of you – a feeling of guilt. Though you have now passed the age of thirty because of your father your hopes for marriage have been twice destroyed and you have not been able to find a job in the business world.

A father's task in South Korea was to arrange for his sons a decent marriage and a decent career.

The letter is sincere and touching but it would be the strange father of a 30-year-old today in the West who would write a similar letter. (Incidentally, now that Kim is the President of South Korea, his son seems to have less trouble finding work.)

Five-star fathers

The little research done up to 1990 suggested that, at best, British attitudes were changing very slowly. In a review of the *Parent Infant Relationship*, Harvey (1980) noted fathers were more likely than ever before to attend the birth and that fathers often saw this as a 'peak' experience. Fathers who were in at the birth were more likely to be more involved with their children. Yet how involved really? Fathers did not wash, feed or change children much at all.

Lummis (1982) took oral histories of Norfolk families and found that fathers were more active role in family life than might have been supposed. But most of their activities Lummis classed as either entertainment or discipline. On average, a quarter of the time mothers spend with infants is play; with fathers 40% of time is spent in play. Though he has apparently changed his views since, in 1987 Charlie Lewis suggested men spend more time

Love in a cold climate. If only all pas were like penguins!

playing because playing is more fun and less work. An unflattering picture of the father as lazy sod emerges.

In an interesting comparison with Humphries and Gordon's snapshot of the 1900–1950 period, Kilpatrick and Trew (1985) looked at unemployed men in Ulster; in theory these men had more time to spend with their children but that did not seem to affect the hours they spent with their children that much. They found that unemployed men spent on average no more time with their children and did not take on more childcare than those men who worked. Again that unflattering picture of the lazy sod dad.

Only in the 1990s, with the often derided 'New Man', did fathers start to take a more active role in childcare. And even on that studies are divided – and it is striking that while there are four national magazines in the UK aimed at parents, there is not one aimed at fathers. I have analysed the photographs and articles published in 2001 in two parenting magazines. The results put men in their place:

- articles directly aimed at mother 76%;
- articles aimed at both parents 24%;
- articles just aimed at fathers 0%;
- pictures of father with child 11%;
- pictures of mother with child 78%;
- pictures of both parents with child 6%.

The natural father

One interesting approach has been developed by psychologists like Blendis (1988). A mixture of survey evidence and history leads them to suggest there are four types of father.

The absent father

He is indifferent and takes little part in the development of his children. Ironically, some men who see themselves as perfectly good fathers are not just absent but over 5,000 miles away from their children. Chris, a 30-year-old estate agent, told me that after spending some £100,000 profits he had made out of property – mainly on drugs – he went on holiday to a French island called Reunion in the Indian Ocean. There, he married an 18-year-old girl. She had his child who is, Chris assured me, 'a wonderful boy.' Only Chris is now back wheeling and dealing in London while his child is in Reunion.

The traditional father

He protects his family but believes in the traditional division of labour between men and women. Blendis found many men in the 1980s remembered their fathers as being of this sort. Unemotional, a little dour, these were men who would never have dreamed of getting involved in any of the dirtier tasks of child minding. One man told Blendis that his father never cuddled him. Another told her of his anger when his father died and regretted; 'I don't think I showed him sufficient love. I don't think I knew how to. I have always wished I had loved him more and that he should have felt it.' It was an unresolved relationship.

The more modern father

He sees that men should do more and, indeed, is willing to do more but, somehow, the theory is always better than the practice. The modern father will play more with children and is willing to take on some childcare tasks as long as they don't interfere with his normal routines too much. He is not totally committed to his children in the way that women have had to be down the ages.

The five-star father

He who is willing to make real sacrifices to help bring up the children and who is passionately committed to child-care. The latter remain rare, Blendis claimed back in 1988. Charles Lewis (2001) claims more modern fathers are behaving like this, though it is still a small number.

And sometimes the literature makes you feel dads will always be in the doghouse. Rosalind Miles heads her chapter on the Father Almighty with Joe Orton's snappy, 'It's all that any reasonable child can expect if the dad is present at the conception.' Is a brilliant quote from a brilliant 'queer', as Orton called himself, really the last word on what all men feel about being fathers?

But I've had my own doghouse experience. Writing on Father's Day 1985 in the *Observer*, I made a plea for men to take on more chores and childcare and enjoy the pleasures of fatherhood. I wasn't suggesting I was a saint, but I didn't expect to be attacked. No less a writer than Katherine Whitehorn wrote a counter-piece arguing that I wanted to rob women of the one area of life where they were in charge.

Savvy kids

It is not just feminism, however, that has triggered changes in the father–child relationship. The consumer pressures which many people deplore are producing unexpected side-effects. In 2000, I went to a number of focus groups with children aged 9–12 carried out by advertising agencies like McCann Erickson. The discussions in the groups suggest families are becoming more democratic. Children expect to be involved in some surprisingly major decisions like buying furniture, computers and, even, cars. In some families, a sharp 10-year-old knows more about information technology and other high-tech gizmos than the parents do. As a result, some parents listen to what they have to say. No one is very sure how often this happens. Robin Laufer who runs *Pulse*, part of McCanns that is dedicated to understanding consumers, detects a major social trend here, however.

Domestic violence and involvement

Contemporary debates on fathering have to take account of the problem, and reality, of child abuse. Since the 1970s, Britain and America have seen a succession of scandals where men, and sometimes, women have abused children physically or sexually. It is notoriously difficult to get accurate figures on the extent of child abuse. Corby (2000) argues the figures show anything between 7% and 29% of women in different countries say they were abused. The National Society for the Prevention of Cruelty to Children point out 36,000 children in England and Wales are officially on the child-protection register. Forty babies a year are murdered, usually by their parents.

In America, reported cases of child abuse have risen from 400,000 in the 1970s to almost 3 million a year. 52% of the victims suffer emotional neglect; 25% suffer physical abuse; 13% suffer sexual abuse. Most of the physical and sexual abuse is committed by fathers and stepfathers, though in Britain one-third of all sexual

abuse is committed by boys under 18, boys who usually
were abused themselves.

Again, we have a paradox. Fathers are more involved
with their children than ever before. At the same time,
there are more cases of violence by fathers against children
than ever before.

Why do fathers abuse children? There are many
theories, none totally convincing. It's a response to
stress, men love the power, all men are rapists. Any
proper analysis has to deal with the role of alcohol
which makes men far less inhibited. I also want to
suggest there is one cause which has not been much
studied yet. This is not to excuse but to explain and we
badly need explanations of abuse which lead to preventing
it.

Some violent men see their victims just as objects; in
other cases, the men are the very opposite of this cold
objective menace. Some dramatic cases of 'family wipe-
out syndrome' (when a man kills his wife, children and
then himself) suggest violent men often have a very poor
sense of boundaries (Palermo and Ross, 1999). They are
almost too involved. Is it possible that some acts of violence against children are not acts of cold callous hatred
but – the paradox – partly the result of men being more
involved with their children? The men don't have the
emotional skills to cope with their own feelings in
certain crises like losing their jobs, or suspecting their
wife is having an affair. They 'console' themselves
through abuse, persuading themselves they are victims
and have the right to fight back.

I cannot answer this important question but what I
can offer, in Chapter 5, is evidence on how angry fathers
should learn to defuse and manage their anger.

It would be wrong to end this chapter on a down note,
however. Usually, fathers love their children and do not
assault them. Fathers have usually taught their children

not just to be imitations of themselves. Fathers have usually, in part, conquered their ambivalances. Often, fathers have been very poor at expressing their love and that has hurt their children. When his father was dying, the poet Dylan Thomas wrote:

And you my father there on the sad height,
Curse, bless, me now with your fierce tears I pray
Do not go gentle into that good night
Rage, rage against the dying of the light.

You can't have a better farewell than that from your children.

2

I'm going to be a dad

Boris Becker recently settled a paternity case. After losing at his last Wimbledon, he got drunk and now admits he had sex with a total stranger. When he was trying to fight the case, however, he claimed she gave him a handjob in a broom cupboard and impregnated herself with his sperm. Faced with the DNA evidence and an apparent crisis of conscience, Becker changed his tune. He has now accepted the child is his and settled for £3 million with the mother. He will support the child. Between Borg and Becker, there is clearly a book to be written on sex and tennis.

History is full of men who borg and disappear. The UN journal, *Development*, argues that in Jamaica men only visit their children if they are guaranteed a borg by the mother. Richard Dawkins in his classic, *The Selfish Gene*, argues this is normal behaviour. Jamaican men are obeying the biological imperative. Their genes want to survive. The more you spread your genes, the more likely that in 3000 AD, your DNA will still be on the planet.

Critics argue that people don't behave entirely as the theory predicts. And the way men respond when they learn they are going to be a father shows it. Many men do feel triumphant. Yes, my genes are in the running for 3000 AD, it shows I'm a real man. But the news can also trigger a conflicting set of feelings – happiness, anxiety, fear that we won't be up to the task. It's an area that has been rather little researched. However, we do know that 40% of men feel they don't get the information they want about what will happen during pregnancy and birth (Singh and Newburn, 2000).

What you feel will be very different depending on whether you are happy with the woman who is bearing your child, or whether you are in conflict about that relationship. Understanding how you feel about these, excuse the word, 'issues', is part of the preparation for being a father.

Western governments today all preach the father is important. The family that stays together doesn't produce those teenage criminals who cost so much to jail. Still, few governments are ready to offer fathers much practical support. In Britain and America, there are still no absolute rights to paternity leave. In one study, only 39% of men got any such leave and most new dads got a princely 2–5 days. Antenatal classes aren't free in Britain; a course will cost at least £80, not an insignificant sum for many families. In France, a new law has been proposed giving men 14 days paid paternity leave but the Minister of Children is now arguing it's a bad idea. Only the Scandinavian countries are more generous and, ironically, that does not seem to encourage men to borg and become fathers.

The evidence is clear though. The father shouldn't be there just at the conception, like Joe Orton seemed to believe. If the father is involved during the pregnancy and the birth, it helps the mother and baby. Women whose partners are prepared for birth and delivery have less pain, take less medication and feel more positive about the birth experience than women whose partners stay aloof.

The ignorant father

Most fathers are not likely, however, to pick up knowledge about pregnancy or babies from their own fathers because father–son relations tend to avoid such emotional intimacies. Blendis (1988) asked men how they felt about their own fathers. Were their basic memories of a warm or a distant relationship? Her sample was small – 31 men in her first study and 119 in her second one. Of the first 31, only 3 had truly positive memories. Of the second sample, only around 28 reported good relationships with their fathers. No one said their father had helped prepare them for being a father.

My own father had small children by his second marriage when I became a father, but he never said anything to me that was helpful. He loved the Bible and I would have rather liked to discuss the implications of the Abraham–Isaac story with him. But the only practical advice he gave me was, first, 'you have to honour the mother of your children' – he had spent years locked in a bitter divorce dispute with my mother at the time – second 'make sure they go to a decent school.' My father-in-law died when our eldest son was four and his younger brother had just been born. He loved his grandchildren, but said nothing of the slightest practical use to me about fathering either.

This silence about fathering from our own fathers is mirrored by relative silence in the literature. I have searched the databases for research on fatherhood and can find surprisingly little. The British Library catalogue lists 1,386 entries under father but only 50 deal with father–child relationships. The rest are theological works about the Bible and America's founding fathers. Also many of the 50 texts on father–child relationships are written by women.

The government helps

In theory, policy is changing. In 2000, a National Institute of Parenting was set up in Britain to provide information about how to be a good mum and dad. The National Childbirth Trust also provide leaflets for fathers, but could not point me to one organisation which helps fathers. There are small groups like Fathers Direct and DIY Dads which promote courses and there have even been courses on how to be a father run in prisons like Retford. But these very recent efforts don't seem to be having that much of an impact yet.

The National Childbirth Trust, in a substantial survey of 817 new fathers (Singh and Newburn, 2000), found that 'more than two-fifths of men' wanted to have more information about topics that ranged from mood swings to how to cope with the baby crying, to sex after childbirth. The survey added; 'There are significant gaps between the information men want about pregnancy, birth and life with a new baby and what they are able to find out.' The survey also noted that 'women are men's main source of information about pregnancy, birth and postnatal issues.'

Of course, some of us fall in love with our children the moment we see or hold them; of course, we want to protect them, but few men have been prepared for this moment. The human father is not Masson's wonder penguin. If we become good fathers, it is very much through our own experiences and, usually, without much help from our friends.

Forget conception. The real drama starts the moment a man is told 'I'm pregnant ... it's your baby ...'

'You're pregnant? – how do I feel?'

Many women worry that their men are not ready to become a father. Joan was 27 years old and married to an accountant whose passion was playing football. She wanted to have a child badly but he kept on delaying. What he often said was that he was not ready and that it would interfere with his sporting career. She felt her biological clock ticking away. In the end, they did not have a child and the marriage ended rather bitterly.

Joan told me she suspected that if she had just gotten pregnant, Tony would have accepted it, but she did not want to force the decision on him.

Joan grasped one point, and suffered for it. If you are a father, you have to stop being a child. You stop being a child because you have a child. And many men don't want to do that yet.

There are two reasons why it is exasperating to find so little research on how men react when they first learn they are to be a father. First, how you react when you as a man learn that a woman is carrying your child is a central moment in human experience. My late mother-in-law, Aileen Blong La Tourette once said 'your children are your immortality', and she was right. When you find out a woman is carrying your child, she is offering you the only true immortality. How you respond at that moment can make or break a relationship. There aren't many, if any, comparable moments between a man and a woman.

One of the men I interviewed told me he felt that Beth was trying to trap him into marriage. He was only 25 at the time. He had a promising career in the City and he didn't want to be tied down by a child. He liked Beth but he insisted they talked about the possibility of her having an abortion. She too had a career, she reminded him. She was quite willing to put that on hold. The word abortion made her furious. The relationship ended bitterly at the time. He felt guilty. Eventually, they did get back together again. Beth had the child but the relationship did not survive for long. The damage had been too great.

Having a child can be, and can make, an enormous bond. Film-maker David Carr Brown was 22 years old when he first learned he was going to be a father. He didn't feel particularly elated. He had moved from Britain where he had been a hospital porter to France where he started to do camerawork. His wife was a florist. Having a child felt just utterly normal. Twenty years later, David is immensely proud of his daughter, Alexandra.

You never wanted my child

The trouble is, in many cases, men don't know what they feel about becoming a father. One way of handling the uncertainty is perhaps the least bad option. You can admit you are nervous. Becoming a father is a huge change. There's no shame in being anxious about it and there is a chance that someone who loves you will understand your own anxieties. It even may help her talk about hers. You can probe and explore what you both find frightening. But remember it's her body that is carrying your child and she will need to talk.

Men being sensitive in this situation is not revolutionary. In *The Care of the Young Baby* published in 1950 when society expected little of fathers, Dr John Gibbens argued the husband must be attentive to his wife. He had to understand and put up with her moods. He had to know it was normal for pregnant women to develop strange appetites for toffee apples and shellfish. Most of all, he had to be there for her. She would probably get very tired and very ratty, Gibbens said. For the moment, however, she needed him as never before, and so would her child. Gibbens seems to have had little influence on the culture of the 1950s or 1960s, however.

We need to return to ambivalence – not between fathers and sons but between fathers and babies in the womb. Sometimes, women are surprisingly accepting of father's indecision. Geraldine was in her early 30s when she got pregnant. She had recently started a new relationship with a man who had children with his wife. He had walked out on his own marriage but was very ambivalent about having more children. Frank told Geraldine he did not want more children. She loved him and understood his reasons for not wanting to be a father again. She is a successful career woman and is now getting on with being a single mother. She has not broken off with Frank because she loves him, because she hopes he will come round to the idea of being the active father of her child and because she is happy to be having a child.

Long term difficulties are most likely either if, as a man, you want to avoid talking about it – she's pregnant that's her problem – or, obviously, if you fundamentally reject the idea of becoming a father. Most psychotherapists say the mother identifies totally with the child she is carrying. Reject the child and you reject her. There are no clever ways round that simple, brutal fact.

If you really hate the idea of being a father, you should at least ask yourself why. A tough question as the answer will touch on your sense of who you are, your relationship to your father, your relationship to your mother and your relationship with the mother-to-be.

The process of pregnancy

During the pregnancy, parents need to dream about and get used to the baby to come. Terry Brazelton, an American paediatrician, argues that for 9 months the pregnant woman lives with her image of the baby in her womb. Men also have images of their future child, especially of sons, Brazelton claims. And that image means fathers can start getting attached to the child before it is born. Key moments are when, after 3 or 4 months, the woman first feels the butterfly movements of the embryo and, then, dad can put his hands on her stomach and feel the creature they have made kicking. The National Childbirth Trust survey reported that most men had seen, and been excited by seeing, ultrasound scans of their child. One man told the survey 'it was quite magical.'

But the National Childbirth Trust survey also identified many practical problems. A third of men were unable to attend antenatal classes because of work commitments. 10% had no idea there were antenatal classes men could attend. Younger fathers aged between 15 and 19 were embarrassed by the idea of attending. A third of the men who did attend antenatal appointments felt they were totally ignored by doctors and midwives.

Antenatal classes stress the importance of the mother staying fit during the 9 months. And that means giving up smoking and alcohol. Ernst (2001) reviews a devastating body of evidence. Mothers who smoke give birth to babies who weigh less. Smoking also affects cell growth in the foetus and the babies of mothers who smoke do less well at school. Ernst has traced studies which show exceptionally long-lasting effects. One study of 1,377 Canadian babies found a link between having a mother who smoked during the pregnancy and having a criminal record 16 years later.

The evidence is so strong that if the mother does not want to give up, the man should do his best to persuade her to do so. That can be rough for both of you, but the evidence can no longer be argued with. Fathers-to-be also need to give up smoking. Ernst shows any exposure to smoke harms the baby. You will also have to help the mother through the withdrawal changes. Fun!

Sex

Sex may also become an issue. Miles suggests many women do not want to have sex while they are pregnant. They see their body as theirs and the child's. Dad is not wanted. Keep out. On the other hand, some women become far randier during pregnancy because their bodies are awash with hormones. Some women love the idea of making love with the father of the child so that their baby is bathed in their fluids. As a man, you must accept the woman's wishes. Nagging your pregnant wife to have sex is storing up trouble.

The run-up to the birth

The National Childbirth Trust produces what it calls a 'birth plan' which 'gives you and your partner the chance to think about labour and the birth of your baby.' The focus is on the mother, but the leaflets do, at least, suggest she discusses with the father:

- where you want to have the baby;
- who you want with you at the birth;
- ways you can help yourself to feel more comfortable;
- pain relief you can ask for;
- monitoring your baby's progress;
- your baby's first hours;
- feeding your baby.

It's a pity the birth plan doesn't also ask couples to think specifically about what the man can do to help the mother and to prepare for the baby. The National Childbirth Trust's survey of 817 men found that nearly 40% had anxieties about the mother's health during the pregnancy.

When I started on this book, my friend Andy was waiting to become a father. He was worried about the health of his partner, Sha. 'Sha doesn't like the idea of pain,' Andy told me. She might have an unusual liver complaint. Doctors told Andy and Sha that it might be necessary to induce the birth which neither of them wanted. 'It's up to Sha,' he said. To add to stress, they were sure the date the doctors gave for the birth was wrong.

Andy's mother is a nurse 'and she says that it's ridiculous to say humans carry babies for 9 months. After all it's a lunar cycle.' So Andy and Sha recalculated and came to the conclusion that, if she was going to be induced, it should be about a week later than the doctors wanted.

Andy and Sha decided to have a second opinion because they were nervous about the child being induced. Also, Andy, a fourth child, had been born at home and wanted his child born at home. Andy coped with the stress well because he was so pleased Sha was expecting. 'I always had the feeling it would be all right,' he told me. And it was. There was no liver problem, fortunately, and 24 hours before the doctors said they would induce the baby, Sha started to have contractions. But even though they attended antenatal classes, they had not had all the information they needed.

'No one had told us that you could have contractions and then they would become less intense. So, we rang the midwife who told us not to be too worried. Then, we fell asleep and I was woken by a blood-curdling scream, as were all the neighbours.' Sha's waters had broken. 'I started to make all the preparations and the midwife only got there about 20 minutes before the baby was born.'

Andy held his daughter Grace within 2 minutes of her being born. 'I felt not so much elated as just out of it for the next 5 to 6 days. I concentrated on the practicalities.'

David Carr Brown was also present at the birth of his first daughter. 'It was a pretty tough labour and about 2 hours before she gave birth, my wife literally fainted. I had been a hospital porter in Guildford and so I had been around such scenes. In addition, the baby was pointing the wrong way. Her feet were coming out first.' David found himself helping the nurse. 'She was pulling on the feet and I was helping push the baby out.'

'When my daughter Alexandra was born, the nurse gave her to me to hold because I was there,' he told me.

David's second child was born 9 years later, in different circumstances. He had left his wife and met Murielle who would become his second wife. She only discovered she was pregnant when she was already 4 months gone. 'The French pride themselves on their medical services but one day she got a letter from the hospital, where she'd gone for something else. The letter said that we are very sorry but, when you came here, we failed to notice the fact that you are pregnant.' It continued to be a dramatic pregnancy.

David and Murielle did not know each other that well. Some 4 months later, he was filming in Italy. The baby was not due for another month when he got a phone call saying Murielle was in labour. 'I got the night train and I made it in time. I was there 2 hours before the birth but she didn't want me to be present. Partly that was because we really didn't know each other that well, and partly because she had to have a Caesarean.'

With their second child, David was in at the birth. 'It was the first time I had deliberately set out to have a child,' he told me, but the experience of being in at the birth was not particularly different. What had changed most was the attitude of the nurses. 'They assumed I knew nothing and when Julian was born they gave him to me to hold, saying it'll be good for you to do that. I suppose I am unusual in that with two of my three children, I held them before their mother did.'

In holding their babies so soon after they were born, both Andy and David were doing just the right thing in terms of attachment theory.

Human bonding

Attachment theory is a key concept in parenting. It is based on the work of the psychoanalyst, John Bowlby, who wrote a seminal paper on 44 juvenile thieves (Bowlby, 1961). Bowlby discovered many of these thieves had been separated from their mothers early in their lives. He argued nature weaves a complex dance between mother and baby. The mother holds and breast-feeds the baby. She provides the first and most basic security. If this bonding, or attachment, does not take place, the baby starts life 'feeling' insecure and that insecurity affects him, or her, for ever. For Bowlby, the father did not matter much.

Yet, fathers speak of holding the baby as being lovely, warm, protective. Some claim that it brings out the often suppressed gentle and feminine side in them. The National Childbirth Trust survey went back to its 817 fathers 6 months after their children were born. Only 53% answered – and these were likely to be men who were most involved with children. Most men said the birth had been a wonderful experience and that they were helping with the childcare, but there were no questions about touching their babies, so again we lack data.

Harvey found that in 1970 that 32% of men held their babies in the hour after delivery. This rose to 50% in the early 1980s. Some psychologists report far less touching. Some research also suggests that even men who do touch their babies are rather timid about it. Usually, they first touch the baby on the feet and toes; today many men are worried about touching babies inappropriately. There is clearly no danger of fathers smotherloving their children to death as Watson feared, except possibly in Africa. The men who hold small children longest are a tribe of Nigerian pygmies called the Akas which may not project the ideal image. Akas, spend 20% of their time holding their children.

Many men are still very diffident about holding babies.

If you feel this way, ask yourself why?

1 Are you afraid of hurting the baby?

2 Are you afraid of uncontrollable feelings?

3 Does it seem somehow wrong or disgusting?

4 Is this the way you feel about small animals?

5 What will alter your feelings?

Being anxious is nothing to be ashamed of. First-time fathers have usually not had much practice holding babies and babies are so small, so fragile. Their skulls still have that terrifying gap where the fontanelles have not yet become solid.

I was lucky. Though I hate touching animals, I was never frightened of holding my babies though I was very conscious of how fragile they were. And I hate cuddling cats, dogs, kittens or the deranged rabbit Benjamin that a woman I once loved allowed to watch television.

But, you can learn. Relax before you pick up the baby. Smile at the baby. Enjoy touching your child. In our anxiety about child abuse, some men are frightened about touching but the sensible way to proceed is not hard to explain. Do not play with the baby's genitals but stroke its head, its arms, its feet. Touching is the best way of developing the bond at first.

Some surprising abilities of the newborn baby

Once, it was believed that the newborn baby was a chaotic confusion of reflexes and brain cells. Psychologists have been unjust to babies. One of the first psychologists to study this was John B Watson (1878–1958). He worked in a clinic in Baltimore and tested hundreds of babies. He found that within 30 minutes of being born babies could turn their heads. He also found that a 14-hour old baby could co-ordinate his movements so as to fixate a light; 3 hours later, the baby could fixate a light that was 20 degrees to the right or left.

Watson's methods of testing were crude. He pinched the baby's nose and then waited to see what the response might be. One indignant baby's hand went up at once and pushed at the experimenter's fingers. Watson believed these were impressive muscular co-ordinations in a newborn. He was also interested in that most powerful of social signals a baby can send – a smile. He saw one instance of a 4-day-old baby smiling. A few other babies smiled on the 7th or 8th day, usually when stroked gently or tickled very lightly.

Myrtle McGraw, a famous Canadian paediatrician, argued that after birth the baby's reflexes are surprisingly well organised. Babies can grasp automatically, for example. Watson had even found the baby can swim or, at least, make reflex swimming movements to keep afloat. McGraw claimed reflexes then become more chaotic and disorganised. On the face of it, this seemed strange, suggesting the baby was suddenly even more helpless. But, it may be that the very fixed instincts of the newborn need to be disorganised, or loosened, because the infant needs a flexible nervous system to get on with the important business of learning and co-ordination.

The abilities of the newborn keep surprising experts. For example, John Morton and colleagues at the Medical Research Council's Cognitive Development Unit, have shown babies recognise their mothers' faces from 4 days of age on. This is a startling fact and the authors admit that they do not quite understand what physiological mechanisms are involved. By 5 weeks, the baby does not have to see the whole face to recognise its mother. In an ingenious set-up, Morton and his team blacked out the shape of the mother's head and her hair. All the babies had to go on were the inner features (i.e. the set of the mouth, the eyes, the nose). By the time babies were 5 weeks old that was enough information for most of them to recognise their mum.

Given his observations, it's curious Watson did not spot that newborn babies have one remarkable skill – they can imitate some actions of adults.

Imitating others ... it starts very young

Such imitation is also the first sign of social awareness. It's worth dissecting what's involved. To imitate what I have just done: first, you have to notice I am there; second, you have to perceive what I have done; third, you have to have the conscious ability to reproduce or parody my actions.

The Swiss psychologist, Jean Piaget (1952) had some nice examples in *Play, Dreams and Imitation*. He suggested the first imitations were vocal. One child T. at 2 months 11 days said la and le. 'I reproduced them. He repeated them seven times out of nine slowly and distinctly.' (p. 9). Piaget thought these first imitations might be just reflexes, but by the age of 4–5 months, he was sure they were signs of intelligence. At 5 months, one of his daughters, J. was definitely imitating him. When he put out his tongue at her, she then put out her tongue at him.

In the 1980s, the evidence became much more dramatic. Meltzoff and Moore (1983) found newborn babies could imitate an adult opening their mouth and sticking out their tongue immediately sometimes. A mere

30-minute-old baby could mimic such actions. This 'skill', the psychologists found, lasted usually till the baby was 21 days. Weirdly, one of the best studies is of Nepalese babies. Reissland (1988) found newborn Nepalese babies could imitate an adult sticking out the tongue, or pursing his lips, or widening his lips.

But when infants were about three weeks old, the researchers found that babies lost this skill. It disappeared as oddly as it had appeared, Then, round 6 months, the ability to imitate was back again.

Why are babies born with this ability to imitate? One possibility is that it is just the kind of endearing behaviour that will motivate adults to bond with and protect them. The baby is rewarding the adult by giving the adult something interesting and moving to respond to. Cuddle me and I'll smile. Do something funny, like poking your tongue out and I'll do something you notice. Rather amazingly, there is evidence that macaque monkeys have a particular class of 'mirroring' neuron which allow baby monkeys to replay some actions they have just seen. This research suggests we may be able to unravel the mechanisms that give human babies these remarkable, slightly disconcerting skills.

Some recent research has tried to work out how quickly babies process information. Babies are trained to respond to stimuli such as triangles or squares. Rather surprisingly perhaps, the results show the baby's brain works at the same speed as the child's brain. The connections function as rapidly as they ever will. But babies cannot concentrate, so they often fail. This is a complicated area of very technical research. In the next chapter, I look at baby memory. But the main point is that babies have more cognitive skills than we used to think. Don't immediately start reading Plato to your 3-month-old, but do provide lots of games, contact and stimulation from the very start.

Try this during your baby's first 24 hours

This obviously suggests a nice game. Stick your tongue out, widen your lips, make utterly silly faces – and see if you can get your baby to make himself look as stupid as you. (We'll assume that the babies aren't being ironic!)

Some babies and small children have to learn practical answers to these fundamental questions. Their brains are well equipped to learn because studies of reaction times show that they process information as fast as 1- and 2-year olds, Kail and Salthouse (1994), Salthouse (1998).

Many fathers do the following automatically, but it's worth spelling out some simple things you can do with your baby which will help bond and also be fun:

1   Make eye contact.

2   Look at your child and smile.

3   Tickle his or her toes. An odd fact is that babies laugh when they are tickled from 2 to 3 months, but we never laugh when we try to tickle ourselves.

4   Test the grasp reflex.

5   Stroke the baby gently.

6   Make ridiculous noises at the baby.

7   Play peekabo, perhaps the most basic of all games. Babies can respond to it by 9 months.

8   Watch for the baby imitating you.

Do not get impatient or scared if the baby cries. Babies do cry. It is their first way of communicating. If your baby never cries, then is the time to be worried because it can be the first sign that the baby is withdrawn.

The safety of the newborn

Since Montaigne's day, when he lost all his children but one before they reached a few months of age, life expectancy has improved. Doctors like to claim it is thanks to the miracles of medicine; sceptics suggest it has more to do with better food and hygiene. Parents worry about the safety of their new baby. This is not a medical textbook, but any father needs to have some sense of the main risks newborns face.

Out of every 1,000 live births in the UK, six babies die. You need to be very vigilant and more hygienic than you normally are. Babies do pick up infections quickly though they are very resilient. Rates in infant mortality in Britain are high by European standards and they are closely related to socio-economic status.

One of the few causes of infant deaths not related to socio-economic status are cot deaths. Studies of cot deaths have been controversial and there are always arguments about particular dangers. The latest view is that it is wise to place the baby on his side when sleeping. Do not put the baby face down. Do not smoke near the baby. Be careful about the mattress you use in the cot.

Share the care

Bringing the baby home from hospital is exciting but also stressful. Fathers can make themselves useful by being attentive and doing some of the essentials. Now is the time to take over the cleaning of where you live. Do the laundry. Do not expect the new mother to cook. Love is practical. When Grace was born, Andy said 'I just focused on the practicalities again.'

Above all, enjoy your new baby. Talk to him or her. Really share the care. The National Childbirth Trust found many men anxious about balancing life and work for very understandable reasons. Employers did not make it easy for men to have much time off. A labourer complained that if he made mistakes, he could be sacked but his wife didn't understand and resented the fact he did not do enough to help. One possibility is to save up holiday entitlements for the birth.

There are also psychological issues. The new mother is also likely to feel obsessed by her new baby, her new love. Many men admit they feel jealous. Blendis found some evidence of this but, again, there seems to be an astonishing lack of precise research.

Do not expect too much attention from the new mother. Also, you will need to be watchful. Most mothers adore their babies and, once they have recovered from the tiredness of pregnancy, enjoy mothering. But some do not. A small percentage do not bond with their babies. Some 15% of mothers develop postnatal depression. Postnatal depression has been recognised as a real condition for centuries and, at the end of the book, I list organisations which provide advice about it.

The obvious thing to do if the mother is weepy, listless and not responding properly to the baby is to seek medical advice. Unfortunately, British GPs remain far too willing to deal with any suffering by just prescribing antidepressants. There has been a sevenfold rise in prescriptions since 1991. If you see the new mother getting depressed, talk to her, go with her to the doctors but do everything you can to persuade her not just to rely on antidepressants.

They can work well in the short term, but they have side effects and people can get as addicted to them as to hard drugs.

Throughout this book, I argue fathers have to be extremely careful about allowing either children or mothers to take antidepressants, sleeping pills or antipsychotic medication because of side effects and the dangers of addiction.

You must also look at whether the way you are behaving – what you are doing and not doing – may not be adding to her stress and depression.

I'd murder for a good night's sleep

Often the most immediate problem is sleep – and here fathers can help even if the mother has decided on 100% breastfeeding.

Lewis (1987) found that looking after a small child in the night was the one task where men did help. 52% of the fathers of 1-year-olds he surveyed said they were involved, though they all admitted the mother did far more. Getting up in the middle of the night to feed your baby is an excellent way of bonding. If the mother is breastfeeding, you can still get up, pick up the baby and bring it to bed, so that the mother is not alone and does not feel this is just her responsibility. If the baby is being part breast part bottle-fed, one of the most sensible times for bottle is in the middle of the night. And dad can do that.

Usually, the baby will be asleep within an hour. I know it can be very exhausting. We used to have a rocking chair and that was a mistake. For a time, our babies only fell asleep while being rocked so always pay attention to what you're doing because you may be creating problems for yourself. Luckily, 21st century technology offers ways of making it more bearable.

Play your favourite music while you are feeding and burping the baby in the middle of the night. If you don't want to wake the mother or the neighbours, wear headphones.

There is the perfect image of 21th century dad – feeding his baby at 3 a.m. wearing headphones listening to Suzanne Vega, Bach or whatever makes you feel good.

The bureaucracy of birth

The child has to be named, registered and, depending on your faith and how religious you are, christened or circumcised. In Britain, a birth has to be registered within 5 days at the local registry office.

If you are Jewish like me, you have to face the question of circumcision. Many think it is a barbaric practice. On the other hand, considerable evidence suggests men who are circumcised are less likely to suffer from some kinds of cancer. Women whose partners are circumcised are less likely to develop uterine cancer. Circumcised fathers face a special problem. Do you want your son's willy to be that radically different from your own? So, parents should perhaps not be put off. Be good to your son's future lovers and have him snipped. It can be done on the National Health and it can be done under anaesthetic.

Pictures are for ever

Your baby will be a newborn only for a short time. Keep a record. Take pictures, take videos. They will be very precious. Andy has already noticed a change during the 17 days of Grace's life. He told me: 'Grace is a very laid-back baby at 17 days. She eats and she sleeps. She's just beginning to take notice of things, just beginning to smile.' Just 17 days old – and already developing.

Andy described Grace like a man in love. Fathers now have to find out just who is this little human they are starting to love.

I have argued earlier that, when a woman tells a man she is carrying his child, it is one of those key moments in life. So is the birth. And she who has just been through it deserves reward.

David Carr Brown's first wife was a florist and that meant 'it was always very important to get the flowers right ... otherwise I was in deep shit,' he told me. There is a lot to thank the new mother for.

Never be afraid of going to the GP and demanding an emergency appointment. If you have a baby or a young child, any responsible surgery will make an appointment quickly available. If the surgery is being difficult, Accident and Emergency departments will generally give babies real priority.

The growth of the mind

By the time they are 4 years old, children can talk, make friends, complain and even tell you what they think you're thinking. They are becoming individual, awkward, loveable, maddening human beings. One of the joys of being a father is watching your children grow and change. We understand far more than ever before about the physical, mental, emotional and social development of babies and infants. A father who understands is better able to nurture, stimulate and protect his children.

The brain can be first identified when the foetus is 3 weeks old; it is a slab of cells in the upper part of the embryo. The brain and spinal cord roll into a hollow cylinder. Between 3 and 4 weeks after conception, brain cells begin to form and multiply around the central hollow; then, the brain cells move to the wall of the cylinder. This cylinder turns into the brain during the pregnancy.

The brain develops far more before birth than any other part of the body. As a result, babies are born with very large heads compared to the rest of their body. At birth, two-thirds of the brain is formed; its structure and anatomy are already very like that of an adult. And now for some brain-boggling figures.

The newborn brain will have roughly 100 billion brain cells. New brain cells do not grow after birth. This fantastic number of cells present at birth form a network that needs to be activated. Textbooks used to compare the brain to a phone exchange. But that analogy sees the brain as very static. Inputs travel along fixed lines to brain cells. The current analogy is that the brain is the greatest, most creative computer we can imagine, a wondrous soft machine with more capacity to learn than trillions of silicon chips.

As the baby starts to see and move, new networks connecting previously unconnected cells are created. Neuropsychologists speak of 'neural networks'. So network X which recognises movement at speed links up with network Q which recognises yellow when the baby sees a yellow mobile above its cot.

One aspect of brain biology highlights the development of connections. After birth, the dendrites, the branches that sprout from the cells, reach out to make contact between brain cells. The points of contact are called synapses (from the Greek work for *clasp*) and, while new brain cells don't form after birth, new synapses form all the time. Researchers use a graphic phrase to describe this process, 'synaptic exuberance'.

Again, we are dealing with brain-boggling figures. Each brain cell is estimated to have an average of 10,000 synapses or connections. Two brain cells will, therefore, have 1 million connections with other brain cells.

With 100 billion cells in the brain, each with perhaps 10,000 connections, mathematicians calculate there are 200,000 times more synapses in one person's brain than there are human beings on Earth. It's hardly surprising we're a bit individual, even quirky.

The biology is mind-boggling; the psychology a little more human and easier to grasp.

The first two stages of development according to Piaget

Work on child development is dominated by the ideas of the Swiss psychologist Jean Piaget (1896–1980). Much of Piaget's work was based on observing his own children, though very often it was his wife Valentine Chatenay who watched and recorded what the babies did. The Piaget children, Jacqueline (born 1925), Lucienne (born 1927) and Laurent (born 1931) were psychological subjects from the moment they were born. Cognitive child development is based to a rather surprising extent on how these three Swiss children grew up in a very different culture a long, long time ago.

I met all three Piaget children at a conference in Lisbon in 1996 held to honour the centenary of their father's birth. Two were still living in Piaget's old house where they had lived as children. They were sweet, deeply devoted to their father's memory, and rather baffled by their role in the history of psychology.

Piaget argued that children's minds develop in four main stages:

1   sensorimotor stage;

2   the preoperational stage;

3   the stage of concrete operations;

4   the stage of formal operations.

By operations Piaget meant logical operations. He was brought up at a time when children were taught formal logic. His theory explains how the baby graduates into a logically competent teenager who can spot the flaws in complex arguments.

Piaget disapproved of what he called the American 'mania' for pushing children, as he thought children's minds develop, or unfold, in an intricate but natural pattern. He often insisted there was not a 'normal' age for a child to go into any of his stages but, inevitably, psychologists have tended to put average ages against the stages.

The sensorimotor stage – roughly from birth to 2 years of age

Piaget did not worry about political correctness in the 1920s and he compared babies to primitive savages! The newborn is a totally confused creature, unaware of the most basic fact of life. When I touch someone, however intimate the touch is, I know where I end and they begin – what is my skin and what is their skin. Babies have to learn this, Piaget found. Babies didn't even know they were a separate being and that their body stopped at the ends of their fingers and the ends of their toes. Beyond that point, the world is other people, other things. The baby 'looks at his own body the way we look at a strange animal', Piaget wrote because 'the baby is submerged in a chaos of interesting impressions without there being any distinction between his internal state and things outside' (1952).

To a father, a baby is both a strange animal and, in some ways, an adorable extension of himself. One of the pleasures of parenthood is witnessing the milestones – the first smile, the first step, the first pull up on the cot.

Try to imagine the questions a baby would ask if a baby could talk:

- What am I?
- What are those things that dance, that make noise?
- Are they different? Are they living?
- Am I living?
- What is out there that is like me?
- Where does out there start and in here end?
- Can I affect it?

Perhaps the very first milestone, the first step to becoming a human being is more subtle.

Meaning to do things

Do you remember the first time you did something you meant to? The first toy you meant to grab, your first deliberate smile? Almost certainly not. Yet, the moment a baby can decide to do something and carries out the act, that baby is on the way to becoming a human being. We cannot imagine a human being who does not intend most of his or her actions. If a murderer pleads diminished responsibility, his lawyer only has to prove his client was so deluded at the time of the killing as not to know what he, or she, was doing just then. What would it be like to be a human being who cannot will his arm to move or his eyes to open?

So, typically, when does a baby carry the first intended action, an action that is not a reflex, like grasping something which just happens to be put in their fingers? Piaget saw the very first traces of these 'intentional' actions from 14 days on. The observations were as follows:

- When Jacqueline was 2 weeks old, Piaget found that if he placed his finger against her cheek, she turned her head and opened her little mouth as if to take the nipple.
- At 23 days, Laurent would search for the nipple with his mouth. If it touched his right cheek, he would turn to the right to look for the nipple.

These actions were not yet intentional, he argued, but they were the first steps in that direction.

Keep a lookout for the first intentional acts, the first smile

By 3 months of age, Piaget's babies were far more co-ordinated. If they heard a noise, they turned their heads to see what might be making it. They stared at objects and reached out for them. According to Piaget, the origins of human intelligence lay in these motor movements, especially in eye–hand co-ordination. This idea suggests fathers should spend time with their babies giving them objects to touch, almost in a very gentle way, teasing them by showing them balls and toys and, then taking them back.

Doing that isn't just a nice game, it is also a way of helping babies discover an important lesson about physical reality.

The truth about objects

For the baby, Piaget claimed, an object is not what an object is for the rest of us. We assume objects are permanent. When I leave my house, I don't worry whether the Hawksmoor Church 50 yards from my front door still exists when I'm not looking at it. I know, of course, it could have burned down while I wasn't looking but, unless there is evidence of a dramatic change, I assume the church still stands. Life would be too chaotic if we didn't make such daily assumptions.

But babies have to learn to make these assumptions. They are completely at the mercy of 'the here and now', at first. If they don't see something, it just does not exist. It has left their universe. Piaget came to his view because he noticed something strange about the behaviour of 6-month-old babies.

Piaget hid objects. Sometimes, the baby saw where Piaget was hiding them; sometimes, the baby didn't. It didn't matter. Once the toy or ball disappeared, the baby behaved as if it had never existed. This was even true when Piaget just draped a cloth over a toy while the baby was looking; the child did not try to remove the cloth. Instead Piaget noted (*The Psychology of Intelligence*, 1950, p. 132) 'the child acts as if the object were reabsorbed into the cloth.'

By the age of 10 month, the baby's behaviour was even more bizarre. When the great psychologist rolled a ball behind cushions, 10-month-old babies did often search for the ball. But they looked in the wrong place. A logical baby would look for the ball behind the cushions but these 'older' babies started looking where the ball had been ... before it disappeared. As if by magic, it might reappear just there.

Some recent research casts some doubt on Piaget's experiments, and he has been criticised for not exploring alternative reasons why babies might fail at some of his tasks. While babies search as he suggests, it has also become clear that babies do follow objects with their eyes, even if they disappear. If a moving object goes behind a screen, babies tend, from 3 months of age, to keep looking further along the path where it should be moving. That does not fit well with the idea that babies 'think' objects drop out of existence the moment they don't see them.

Today, psychologists think Piaget often underestimated what babies could achieve and some research carried out in the 1990s would probably have startled him.

Does memory start in the womb?

Peter Hepper (1991) in Belfast made pregnant women listen to music including the signature tunes of television programmes such as *Neighbours*. And when their babies were born, they responded more to that tune than to other music; our memory systems start to work even before we are born. The foetus must have been able to store the memory of the *Neighbours* tune and then access and retrieve it. And the non-smoking, non-drinking foetus remember tunes better!

The strongest evidence that babies can remember comes from studies by Caroline Rovee Collier at Rutgers University. Since the early 1990s, she has been looking at infants as young as 8 weeks. As babies cannot speak, Rovee Collier has had to be inventive.

If a toddler sees a toy, he or she can whoop 'there again'. The baby cannot say a word but Rovee Collier claims the baby's movements will reflect that same excitement. She uses the rate at which babies kick when they are shown a mobile to work out whether or not they remember. Her logic is simple. If babies remember nothing, then the particular mobile they are looking at will not make any difference to their kick rate. But if they do remember, we should see differences when they are shown a new mobile as opposed to one they have seen before.

First, Rovee Collier trains babies to kick when they see a mobile. She establishes the average kick rate for each baby. Then, she shows the babies either a mobile that displays the same stimuli the baby was 'trained on' or a new one. The rate of kicking 'tells' Rovee Collier whether the babies 'remember'. If they kick more than their average, then that is 'yes, the same', but if they do not kick above the average, then they are saying 'no ... this is any old mobile so I'll kick at my average rate.' Some psychologists dispute the logic of the experiment but Rovee Collier has got impressively consistent results.

Babies as young as 8 weeks will kick far more at a mobile they have seen before than at a new mobile. Three-month-olds show near perfect memory for mobiles several days after training. The results are impressive also because the baby's memory seems to work much like the way adult memory works. If you show adults a set of items, they will remember the first one presented better than the rest. Rovee Collier found this so-called 'primacy effect' also operated with babies. The mobile shown to them first was remembered best. There was one difference though. In adults, it doesn't matter whether you show subjects 3 or 300 stimuli; the first one still has an advantage. With babies that seems to be different. If you show them 5 mobiles, then you do not get the primacy effect.

The reason? A perfectly understandable one, argues Rovee Collier. While babies have the same essential memory system as adults, psychologists impose too much strain when they show them 5 different mobiles. The baby's immature brain cannot handle so much information and suffers from the modern malaise of information overload. As a result, the primacy effect does not function. With 3 mobiles, however, babies can cope and the laws of adult memory, of primacy, work.

Priming and primacy – not the same thing

Rovee Collier has also looked at the effects of priming. Don't confuse your primacy with your priming by the way. The psychological meaning of priming is very similar to the do-it-yourself meaning of priming. It's a question of preparing the ground. In one study, 30 3-month-olds were first trained to kick to a mobile which had an S design on it. Two weeks later, these infants were 'primed'. They were shown the S mobile again but this time the experimenter moved it about instead of it just dangling above their cots.

The next day, the babies kicked significantly above the baseline level when they were shown a mobile with either the original S design, or a larger S, or a smaller S. Rovee Collier claims to have proved 3-month-olds have two memory systems operating – one that only works for stimuli that are identical in size to the one first shown, and one where the size does not matter. Adult memory systems work just like that. Rovee Collier's work is controversial; she and her colleagues complain that 'developmental and cognitive psychologists have resisted conclusions that infants have two functionally distinct memory systems' (Gerhardstein *et al.*, 1999).

This is not a book about the intricate and, sometimes,

heated debates between developmental psychologists, but you don't have to be Freud to see why some critics complain Rovee Collier assumes too much. Does the rate of kicking really relate to memory? Can you tell quite so much from mobiles? I am fairly convinced by Rovee Collier's views and urge dads, and mums, to play the following mobile game with their babies.

Box 2   Mobile games

Show your baby two different mobiles – say a pink one and a striped one with no pink on it. Watch for how much the baby kicks to each mobile. If you feel particularly systematic, time how many kicks occur during 60-seconds. Say they kick 15 times to the pink and 12 to the striped, your baby's average 60-second kick score is 13.5.

The next day, show the baby one of these mobiles – and a brand new one. Count the kicks again. See if there is any difference between the previously presented mobile and the new one. If there is, according to Rovee Collier, you have proved your baby is remembering. You don't have to treat this as a serious scientific exercise. It's a nice game to play, but if you start tickling the baby's feet, you're cheating.

Childhood amnesia

Having a child may well bring back memories of your own childhood – and that prompts an interesting question. If babies can remember, why do we not remember anything of our lives as small children?

Sigmund Freud believed 'childhood amnesia' is caused by psychological conflicts the child faces such as the Oedipus complex in boys. (Young girls have to cope with the Electra complex. Just as boys want to replace their father, young girls hate their mother and want to replace her to get their father's undivided attention.) These fierce emotional and sexual wishes are unconscious. Freud's child has been well enough socialised by the age of 3 or 4 to 'know' these desires are sinful and unrealistic; so the child represses the feelings and, then, suppresses the memories.

It is not easy to get evidence of the unconscious at work but some support comes from Kathleen Nelson who taped the babblings of a toddler called Emily from when she was 16 months old. When Emily's parents were not in the room – and Emily thought she was alone – her speech showed much anxiety and emotion. When Emily could see her parents, however, she babbled less anxiously (Nelson, 1989). Proof perhaps that babies repress something. The late Paul Kline argued Freud's ideas were 'not proven but not totally out of the question.' (Kline, 1972). There could be other explanations though. Maybe these early memory traces are so unstable they literally break up or decompose in the brain; maybe they are buried so deep they cannot be accessed. But those touching moments – your baby's first steps, your infant's first sentence in which he or she uses the words chocolate or Pokemon – you will remember them vividly. But your child won't have the slightest recollection of them.

Learning to speak

All parents wait for their child's first word though few are sharp enough to catch it on the camcorder. There have been reports of children as young as 9 months making a meaningful utterance – saying 'buff', for example, when they see something that moves like a car. On the other hand, Einstein said virtually nothing until he was 4 years old, so you need not panic if your toddler doesn't speak. Equally, don't assume silence means your kid is a cosmic genius. He could just be planning a career as Mr Bean.

Language marks us out from all other species. Attempts to teach chimps sign language shows that at best they achieve the speech of a slow 2-year-old who can say 'Me banana ... want'. The expression 'learning to speak' is slightly inaccurate. We learn but do not learn to speak. Human brains are hard-wired for language. In right-handers, the crucial brain areas responsible for language have long been known to be in the left temporal lobe.

There seems to be a critical period for language learning. Children 'learn' to speak, just as long as they hear language, by a certain point in time. If that does not happen, then the moment passes and the brain structures for learning language do not work. It is not clear whether they actually atrophy, or whether the brain cells just can't set up the connections needed for normal speech. As in much psychology, some key evidence comes from abnormal situations including cases of so-called wolf children or grossly abused kids. Children who have lived wild and are then found seem to have missed the critical period of learning language. The crucial divide seems to be around 7 or 8 years of age. Children who do not hear language by then do not ever seem to speak properly. One wild child was found in Aveyron in France in 1798 and, eventually, taken to Dr Itard who tried hard to teach the boy to speak and failed. Indian missionaries like Singh in the 19th century found two wolf children, and also did not manage to get them to speak normally. The trouble is that, usually, no one knows the age of these 'wolf' children or their early history.

The 'dogboy' found in Chile in the summer of 2001 is different. That child had lived on the streets, been taken into care and run away to live in a cave with a pack of dogs. The boy was deeply disturbed, but he had already learned to speak when he ran away. The basic fact is clear. A child who has lived isolated from human society and who has not learned to speak by the age of 8 will not acquire normal language.

It isn't just these cases that suggest language is innate. In the 1950s, the American linguist Noam Chomsky from MIT showed that all languages have what he called a *deep structure*. This has nothing to do with adverbs or even sentences, but with meanings. He also showed the way children learn language does not conform to the normal laws of learning (Chomsky, 1957, 1986). If these laws operated, children would just utter combinations of words they had already heard. But children do not, when they learn to speak, only repeat words or sentences parents 'teach' them and reward them for speaking. Children consistently produce original sentences, new combinations of words. The language of learning is creative, Chomsky told me in an interview (1977).

Fathers only have to listen to note the evidence. Sometimes, children come out with strange sound combinations and, sometimes, they do just 'create', as a girl called Helen did when seeing a walrus at the zoo. She lay down on the grass and threw herself from one side to the other, saying 'flip flop ... like a walrus'. Good words, but this combination of 'flip flop' and 'walrus' was not a combination she could ever have heard, or been rewarded, for hearing before.

If language is innate, it does not, however, mean parents do not make a contribution. Wells (1981) showed how parents teach children crucial skills involved in talking. You cannot have a conversation without being aware of many non-verbal cues; you need to sense the rhythm of conversation you have, to pause to let others speak; you have to give subtle sound cues to those you are conversing with which tell them you are coming to the end of your utterance. Children whose parents talk to them, repeat things for them and explain the meaning of new words will also have a better vocabulary younger. Parents are useful, but not necessary, when it comes to learning to speak.

Language learning, in fact, is a nice example of how nurture and nature work together. Your children will benefit if you speak to them and read to them and play verbal games with them.

I really don't want to seem a fool

I suspect some (but far from the majority) of fathers experience a particular problem in talking to children. To talk to a toddler, you have to be willing to talk slowly and often childishly. You baby-talk to babies. Yet, when we grow up, we keep on being told not be childish. Yet, here the adult is supposed to be childish. It's not surprising that some men find this hard and so talk less to their children than they might.

The mysteries of mirrors

Just as language is a crucial test of humanity so is being able to recognise yourself in the mirror. Some great apes seem to be able to do that, according to some new research; dolphins also behave differently when they see their own reflection as against that of other dolphins.

The baby usually manages to recognise himself in the mirror by 18 months. When I studied the development of laughter, I showed children in a nursery film of themselves. I was struck by how they responded, often with frantic laughter, when they saw themselves appear on screen. Seeing themselves they became very self-conscious.

The personality of small children

Nicholas' first holiday experience was startling. When he first saw the sea at Calpe in Spain, he gurgled with delight and tried to run straight into it.

Babies who love exploring can also put themselves in danger. At 9 months, Nicholas searched underneath the dining room table for a piece of cake; also searching was his grandparents' dog. Nicholas got the cake but then the dog got his nose. Nicholas had to be rushed to hospital to have plastic surgery and spent his first Christmas among desperately sick children. Five months later, undaunted, he clambered into the oven of the cooker in the villa we had rented in Spain. Then, a scream. He had managed to pull the cooker down on top of himself. Miraculously, he was not hurt. We did not realise it, but Nicholas' readiness to explore meant he would score high on the exuberant side of the exuberance inhibition scale. Some psychologists believe this scale makes it possible to judge a child's personality from 4 months of age (Schmidt and Fox, 1998).

The Greeks, 2000 years ago, argued people were basically calm or fiery. It is odd to find ancient Greek personality theory back in favour. Does the newborn tend to stay still or does he or she explore? Is the baby placid or nervous? In 2001, Lord Winston's TV series on child development figured the tiger test in which a man in a tiger mask appears. Does the baby cry, touch the tiger or just watch? Some argue you need nothing else to work out a child's personality. Schmidt and Fox distinguish between exuberant and inhibited children based on more than the 'tiger test'.

Key factors in exuberance versus withdrawal

These temperamental differences seem to go hand in hand with certain physiological differences, Schmidt and Fox argue. Infants who stay still, become fearful and do not explore much tend to have three distinguishing characteristics. These are:

1   A stable and relatively high heart rate which does not change when challenged.

2   Higher levels of Norepinephrine and, in the morning, Cortisol.

3   An imbalance between the right-hand side and the left-hand side of the brain. It is always difficult to know what differences in brain activity exactly mean, but psychologists have discovered an EEG or EMG asymmetry. Inhibited children seem to have more brain activity in the right hand side of the brain. Some researchers argue that this is related to a structure called the amygdala which is associated

with fear. Put very crudely, if the amygdala is more active, it is easier for people to experience fear. The more active the amygdala, the more likely the infant will be temperamentally more fearful and so less likely to explore.

Recently, some researchers argue that 4-month-old babies are not as fixed in their personality, as Schmidt and Fox claim. The shy and inhibited 4-month-old does not necessarily become a shy and inhibited 4-year-old. Experiences between 4 months and 4 years can change the baby's personality though no one is sure what these personality-changing experiences might be.

What's normal?

For parents, the question of whether your child is developing normally is always a worry. Good enough fathering involves noticing things about your child. It is very normal to feel concerned if a child seems to lag behind or to have great difficulty with particular tasks. But fathers must not panic prematurely. The more we know about child development, the clearer it is that normal children develop at different 'speeds'. Nevertheless, I include the following guidelines without panicking, you should seek advice if by the following ages your child is failing to:

- fix his or her gaze at objects   9 months
- sit up   11 months
- make first attempts to walk   20 months
- speak a few words   30 months

Good enough fathering

Being a parent, wanting to be a good parent, means we put ourselves under pressure. The psychoanalyst D. W. Winnicott argued many mothers tortured themselves with the fear that they were inadequate mothers. They wanted so much to be perfect mothers, they felt guilty about every possible failure.

In the past, men did not really expect to play a part in fathering so they had less reason to feel they were failures. More fathers than ever before want to be involved, so fathers are more likely to feel they should get everything right, providing baby with the perfect cot, the perfect room, the perfect toys, the perfect intimacy.

Some men will be very vulnerable to feel those pressures and all too ready to blame themselves if they think they have failed. Most experts are clear about the basics a baby and a young child needs – and have been clear about them for 75 years.

A child needs:

- a clean bed;
- a clean room;
- proper food;
- while a baby, either breastfeeding or bottles at the right time at the right temperature, or a combination of breast and bottle;
- the chance to grasp and manipulate objects;
- cuddling;
- the chance to play with other children;
- some toys though there is no reason to spend a fortune;
- the presence of mother;
- the presence of father;
- freedom from violence, sexual abuse and neglect;
- emotional security;
- stimulation.

I am sure I could add to the list but these seem basic, practical needs. Give them to a child and that child will feel loved. I have made a list because theorists like Lacan (who believes all fathers are doomed neurotics) and Rosalind Miles (who argues men can't give unconditional love) are so ready to attack fathers. If you start out by giving your baby the essentials on the list, you will be, not the perfect father, but a good enough dad.

And your young child will thrive.

Rats, monkeys and babies who have had good mothering and fathering are more likely to explore new environments. The child who feels loved and safe will have the self-confidence to test what the world is like because he, or she, knows they can scamper quickly back to the safety of home. And fathers play a large role in creating that self-confidence.

A good enough walk in the park

I will never forget walking through Greenwich Park with Nicholas every morning when I was taking him to nursery school. For 30 minutes, we talked as we trotted through the park. I would be lying now, if I said I remembered what we talked about. I suspect it wasn't about the trees since I can barely tell a birch from an oak. But we found endless topics of conversation.

At about 8.30, we would get to the kindergarten behind St Alfege's Church. Some days, I waited till the school opened. Sometimes, I was in a hurry to get to work. As soon as one of the mothers I knew – and it was nearly always mothers – arrived, I asked if she minded taking Nicholas in. Sometimes, he cried as I was leaving and, then, I explained I really had to get my train and I went.

We did this routine most school days for 3 years. Was this perfect fathering? Of course not. The perfect father would have stayed, missed his train, been late for work. Was it good enough fathering? I would say yes. I never left him alone, never left him with an adult I did not know and never left without explaining to him why I had to try and catch the train. I enjoyed every minute of it.

Don't try to be a perfect father. You'll make mistakes. You'll feel angry. You'll wish the little monkey would stop crying in the middle of the night and you'll yell at him to shut up. It seems to me two things are crucial. First, your basic attitude. Do you enjoy your child most of the time? Second, precisely because there will be times you are tired or fed up, stay in control of your feelings. Your child is small, weak and dependent. She, or he, should never have to cope with your bad moods. That's easy to say but takes a lot of self-discipline.

The egocentric child in the preoperational period – 2–7 roughly

A huge amount of research has also concentrated on the child's progress after the age of 2. Between 2 and 7, Piaget claimed, the child still cannot master real logical operations. That's why Piaget called this the preoperational stage. One of its hallmarks is that children are totally egocentric.

Piaget did not use the term *egocentric* in our modern sense. It wasn't a question of being totally selfish or self-obsessed. Preoperational children were egocentric in being unable to perceive how anything might look from anyone else's perspective; they could only hold in their minds what they saw or heard in the here and now.

Piaget proved the point in a number of experiments which are worth outlining.

Peak perspective

Piaget showed 4–6-year-old children a doll and model of three mountains. As the doll was moved about, the children were asked to pick which of a number of photographs represented what the doll was seeing. If the doll was on the highest peak, she'd be looking down at the others. On the lowest, she'd be looking up at the other two.

Four and five year old children nearly always did not manage the perspective test. They couldn't imagine what the mountain view was like from any point of view other than the one they happened to have at that moment.

Ten little buttons

In a second experiment, Piaget showed 4–6 year olds a row of ten buttons. He then set out a second line of ten buttons. He'd then take away one button but stretch the nine button line out so that it was as long as the line with ten buttons had been.

Were there more or fewer or the same number of buttons in this second line? Most children aged 6 said the same number of buttons because the lines were the same length. Again, their immediate perception made them respond illogically; they never counted the actual buttons.

Conservation task

This was one of Piaget's classic experiments. He would show 4–6-year-old children Container B which was filled with water to a certain level. With the children watching, Piaget would then pour the water out of Container B and into Container A. Usually, this container was thinner and longer than the first.

Is there more or less water in A than there was in B, Piaget would ask.

Before they were 7, children nearly always replied there was more water in Container B even though they had seen it was the same water. Not a drop was spilled. Piaget saw this as proof again of the power of immediate perceptions. If Container B looks as if it has more water than Container A, and children under 7 can't remember what was in Container A, and so say there is more water in Container B, they must be victims of 'abusive perceptions', as Piaget put it – and bad memory.

Piaget argued that when children were asked to perform these kinds of task between the ages of 6 and 7 they seemed uneasy. It was as if they had begun to get a glimpse of different ways of seeing things. These 6–7-year-olds began to sense their view of the world wasn't quite in tune with reality, that it was wrong, primitive, illogical. They felt what Piaget called **disequilibrium**. Good teachers and smart parents talked with children about the reasons for that.

Your child's IQ – does it matter?

I have left till last the tangled question of IQ or Intelligence Quotient. Psychologists have been studying children's IQ for a hundred years and it seems to have risen over the century. Lynn (1999) suggests it is partly due to better nutrition. To understand what you can, and can't, expect IQ to tell you about your child demands a trip back in time.

The city of Paris in 1903 wanted to make sure its schools could help children who seemed to be failing. The city authorities asked two French psychologists, Alfred Binet and Theodore Simon to devise a strategy. First, Binet and Simon came up with the idea of measuring **norms of achievement** for different ages. To find the norms, they devised rather quaint lists of tasks for children to do. Four-year-olds, for example, were given instructions to follow; they were told to pick up a key, put it on a chair at one end of the room, shut a door, then pick up a box and bring it back to the experimenter. The child had to remember a sequence of five actions. Most 4-year-olds could not manage it. Half the 5-year-olds succeeded, however.

The average 6-year-old could manage to:

- tell the difference between morning and evening;
- copy the picture of a diamond;
- count 13 pennies;
- distinguish between pictures of ugly and pretty faces;

The normal 8-year-old could manage:

- to compare two objects from memory;
- to count up to 20 without hesitation;
- to say what had been left out of a picture he had just seen;
- to repeat back a list of five digits.

Such questions are at the root of all IQ tests. Seven of the eight questions have a definite right or wrong answer; only distinguishing a pretty from an ugly face allows for any debate. Binet and Simon discovered what was normal for children of different ages and so were able to measure just how able a particular child was in comparison with other children. The IQ test is a comparative measure, not an absolute one. If I weigh 53 kilos that is an absolute measure. I may be light or heavy for my age and height but the 53 kilos is 53 kilos.

IQ scores are relative, comparing a child with the average for his group – not absolute scores.

Binet and Simon's work created the intelligence quotient. And it's worth explaining why it has the name. They would give a series of 20 questions. After a while, they knew that the norm for 6-year-olds was to be able to answer 12 of these questions. If a 6-year-old got 12 out of the 20 questions right, he or she would have an IQ of 100, dead average. A 6-year-old who got 16 questions right, would have an above average IQ. This allowed Binet and Simon and their followers to create the following equation:

The intelligence quotient is: $\dfrac{\text{Mental age}}{\text{Chronological age}} \times 100$

The norm for 8-year-olds was to get 16 questions right. With the 6-year-old child who answered all the questions an 8-year-old should, her IQ score would be:

$$8 \div 6 = 1.25 \times 100 = 125$$

Research from 1903 to 1960 showed that only 4 children in 1,000 have an IQ of above 140. Einstein's IQ has been reckoned at above 180.

It is easy for parents to get obsessed about their child's IQ, but it's not particularly smart for a number of reasons.

First, IQ tests only test one particular kind of intelligence. They tell you nothing about imagination, or creativity, or 'contrary imaginations', as Liam Hudson called them (Hudson, 1966). Second, children come under pressure at school soon enough. Third, there is no evidence that having a high IQ predicts a great future. The late Hans Eysenck, a great fan of tests, told me wryly he had noticed members of MENSA (an organisation that you can only join if you have an IQ of 140 or above) were neither particularly rich nor particularly successful. In fact, their main and, often only, claim to fame was having a high IQ. Eysenck had come to see they did well at school, but often that was the height of their achievement. To do well in life you need personality, persistence, other kinds of thinking.

IQ tests are only important if you begin to worry your children may be very slow – and in this case they can be a diagnostic tool. But if you fear that, you should take them to see an educational psychologist, not get involved in DIY testing. And before you do that, see how they respond to tender and intelligent loving care. Two most useful things fathers can do with their children is to talk to them and read to them.

Read, read, read

There are better and brighter books for very young children on the market now than ever before, ranging from the still magical Dr Seuss books to Postman Pat.

One of the reasons Seuss is so successful is that most children love rhymes and there is much research which links readiness to read with the ability to make and understand rhymes.

One of the simplest of games for fathers to play with their children is the rhyming game (Box 3).

Box 3   Rhyme for a time ...

The rhyming game does not take hours. You can devote 5–10 minutes an evening to questions like this which you can put to your children – and laugh with them about.

1   Which kind of jam do you want for your ram?

- Bam jam?
- Sam jam?
- Zam jam?

2   What animal rhymes with fuss?

3   Complete the following verse:

> *You'll get my vote*
> *If you float*

answers to (2) include walrus, hippopotamus. Answers to (3) include a goat in a boat, a groat in a boat, a stoat in a boat and an oat in a boat.

As in many games, to get in the spirit, fathers have to be willing to be totally childish.

Silly photographs – an important bonding tool!

Most parents have a sentimental streak about their own children. But you won't have anything to be sentimental about if you don't collect material at the right time. Take pictures of your children, show them to them and talk about the pictures with your small kids. No research proves what effect this will have, but it is likely to help you bond – especially if dad is wearing an absurd hat and making silly faces.

And while my genes hope to make it to 3,000 AD, I hope photos of me and my children and their mother also make it to around 2,200 AD. After that, posterity gets a bit theoretical.

My daughter is a princess, my son is a genius ...

A final plea. It is utterly normal for parents to want their children to be normal and to shine. Remember though that history is full of geniuses who developed late. Winston Churchill hated school, was thought something of an idiot and yet he did more to save the world than anyone else.

Pretending, playing and lying

In *The Development of Play*, I argued adults often lose the capacity to play with – and this is I hope the only time I use the phrase – 'the innocence of childhood.' The extent of bullying in playgrounds shows how naive that phrase is. Children play funny, clever, sweet and sometimes nasty games. They switch in and out, fast as a lizard, between the fantastic, the frivolous and the serious and, in doing so, they test themselves, their peers and their parents.

When adults play, they tend to be playing something with established rules, football, poker or bingo. Child's play doesn't have such rules, though by the age of 4 normal children know the limits. You can't hit other children really hard when playing because hard hitting is not really play. Grown men have their rules too, and they exclude scampering on the floor making noises like an elephant. Yet being Jumbo is often fun, an excellent way of bonding with your kid and de-stressing yourself after a tough day in the so-called real world.

Twenty years ago, two American psychologists Curry and Arnaud sketched the typical play of the typical

2-year-old, the typical 3-year-old and so on. Two-year olds played with toys, but did not yet play with other children. They watched other children carefully and often imitated them, but they did not have the social skills to play with them. The collaboration needed to play cowboys and Indians or cops and robbers was too much at that age.

Three-year-olds started to play with each other, but Curry and Arnaud found they could be very bossy. It was only when the toddlers reached the age of 4 that they started to play real games together. Curry and Arnaud found four is also an age which seems to mark an important shift towards becoming a micro human. Four-year-olds were attuned to each other; they knew perfectly well what another child liked or hated so they could play co-operatively, or the little monsters could do their best to upset their 'playmates'.

In the Greenwich playground where I observed what made children laugh, I recorded scenes like this which show the complexity of pretending. R pretends to pour Daniel a cup from the kettle saying 'yes sir'. Daniel giggles. Daniel dives under the table in the Wendy House, gets up, places a cup on his head and says 'Hello hello'. The cup then clatters on the table and he laughs. A moment later, R pretends to pour tea from the kettle into a cup and chuckles. He 'then' feeds Jamie from the spout and he and Daniel laugh. Miming is also often accompanied by laughter.

These 3–4 year-olds were well aware of other children and played with them. Pretend play has become a hot topic in psychology because the ability to pretend seems to enable children to learn a number of essential social and emotional skills and truths, especially that 'moi' is not the only person in the universe.

The birth of a pretender

It is as difficult to be sure when children start to pretend play as it is to know when they first smile. By the time they are 15 months old, most children will show some pretending behaviours. Psychologists like McCune-Nicolich, Judy Dunn, Paul Harris, and literally hundreds of others have looked at the development of pretending in enormous detail since the 1980s. In the section that follows, I map out what research shows about children on average. Averages are only guides. Your own child may be different and pretend more or less.

Infants don't immediately start to pretend they are Superman or Lara Croft. Most children will first pretend by carrying out an action where something vital is missing. Often, they pretend to eat even though there is no food. The infant will take an empty spoon up to the mouth and make all the mouth movements that normally accompany eating. Or she or he will pretend to eat their fingers. Twelve-month-olds also often pretend to drink.

Next, the child will pretend to feed another person – mother, father or a sibling – or a doll. The child takes an empty spoon and brings it up to the doll's mouth. At first, the doll is just the passive recipient of food. But, then, most infants start to play games in which they give the doll 'life' so that they sometimes feed the doll and act out the doll's response. The doll loves or hates the food, she says yuck or yummy spaghetti.

The earliest pretence I saw was when one of my sons ran around the living room yelling 'I'm Batman' and put a cape round his shoulders. He was 18 months old and I wondered. Did he realise what he was doing? Was there a corner of his mind which knew perfectly well, as an actor or a 6-year-old would, that he was not really Batman. It's hard to be sure. By the time he was 3, he certainly knew when he rushed about as Fantastic Man really, that, he was not this self-invented superhero. He could explain some of the differences between himself and Fantastic Man; he couldn't really fly and didn't have Fantastic Man's magic powers.

Curry and Arnaud also found 3- and 4-year-olds often pretended to be aggressive superheroes or monsters. Chases were common. But the children's imagination was stuck with sex roles. Girls did not play Superman. The boys played with guns and the girls played with dolls. Lara Croft may have changed it a bit now, but researchers tend to lament how sex-stereotyped play is.

I observed many long sequences of pretending games with my children. My younger son was fascinated by Batman when he was 2, and he soon worked the characters into his chases. Two months later on, he could imagine himself playing a part as he chased smiling as he said 'Superman ... I fly' and ran around the living room. He also often rushed round the room saying he was Aquaman or Fantastic Man. But the most original character he ever devised was a saga in which he assumed the role of a flying cucumber; his performance as the aerodynamic veg held us all spellbound for 15 minutes.

Dad as playmaster

I was, of course, not just being a father playing with my children. I was a father who was playing with the children and studying for his PhD, so I was play working or work playing. Fathers need to give time to playing with their children even when the children aren't research subjects. I was, at least, willing to appear a perfect idiot. I didn't find that hard even, though I cannot ever remember my father doing anything of the sort with me. His style was more James Mill. He took me to the Old Vic when I was 10 and expected me to discuss *Richard II* and *The Importance of Being Earnest* critically.

Box 4   Inhibited? Frightened of seeming a total moron?

Do you believe men who crawl on the carpet get taken to loony bins? If so, I recommend the following, only to be done after work. Anticipated reward; classy cocktail, Bounty Bar or your favourite food, 500+ calories of pure indulgence:

- Go to the mirror.
- Remove all your clothes apart from your underpants.
- Stick your arms out. Try to look like a tree.
- Admit you don't do a very good tree. Tickle yourself under the armpits.
- Ask yourself why you do not laugh when you tickle yourself (this question has actually puzzled laughter researchers).
- Gaze at the human form in the mirror and repeat 'I come from a long family of Neanderthals ... 25,000 years ago my ancestors roamed the savannah in loin cloths.'
- Yes I am ridiculous. Life is ridiculous. I am happy to be ridiculous.'
- 'If experts recommend I crawl on the carpet

> making trunk noises like an elephant, the chil-
> dren come first. Watch out Jumbo is coming.'
> - Put on some of your clothes before re-joining
>   your family or the neighbours.

The ability to pretend is also intimately linked to sophisticated aspects of cognitive development. Not yours, the
child's.

Lying, pretending and false beliefs

Philosophers distinguish between knowing how and
knowing that. I know how to talk but I do not know
that, that being the intricacies of grammar. Research suggests, however, children understand more than we used to
imagine of what we might call the grammar of pretending.
Harris, Kavanaugh and colleagues studied how children
understand pretending from the age of 17 months to 57
months. Some children seemed to get the idea as early as
18 months.

At 29 months of age, most children could understand
what Harris and his colleagues call the pretend frame-
work. If, for example, experimenters poured pretend tea
over a duck, children aged 29–30 months would say the
duck was wet. In fact, no tea had been poured; the duck
was as dry as before. But the children understood the
spirit and the point of the game. So, they said, the duck
was now wet. A few months later, the children realised
that just as they could pretend, a doll could pretend the
duck was wet – and they could make a doll pretend. The
convolutions are endless.

It is really strange, given that society sees pretending as silly, that it seems to be an essential ingredient in intellectual and social development. Somewhere between 3 and 4 years of age, the child who can play the ordinary pretend games I've described makes a quantum leap.

My child is a real person – what do I do now?

Between 3 and 5, children discover other people have other ideas, other feelings and, what philosophers call other minds, a sense of other people. In 36 short months, they have grown from Piaget's chaotic confusion to an almost person – and the evidence is to be found in their everyday speech.

Psychologists have looked at when small children start to talk about common mental states like believing, hoping, liking, desiring. A mental state cannot be observed. It is inside your mind. So psychologists have observed external behaviours; for example, when infants begin to use verbs that reflect mental states. We assume that when a toddler says 'I want', 'I think', 'I believe', 'I wish', 'I dream', 'I like' and so on, he or she is expressing the fact they're experiencing the relevant mental state of wanting, believing or dreaming.

At the University of Michigan, Henry Wellman and his colleague Karen Bartsch have analysed some 200,000 conversations between children, their parents and sometimes other adults. They followed a small sample of ten children for $4\frac{1}{2}$ years. To parents, many of the following conversations with 4-year-olds that Wellman and Bartsch record will feel familiar:

Ross (3.10*): *Leslie makes me angry.*

Adult: *Why?*

Ross: *If she thinks something is silly. I don't think it's silly at all.*

Adult: *Oh, you had a disagreement.*

Ross: *Uh huh, She thought her necklace was silly.*

Adult: *She thought it was silly?*

Ross: *Yeah. But I didn't think it was.*

Ross clearly understands Leslie has a mind of her own, and what Leslie is thinking is not what she is thinking. When the adult asks tough questions, Ross has nothing to hide and explains the situation well. He and Leslie disagree about the necklace. When the adult explains what he thinks Ross thought about Leslie's ideas about the necklace, Ross gives a perfectly sensible, perfectly adult answer. He and Leslie have different thoughts and feelings about the necklace.

Young children tend to talk more when talking with their parents. One child was just 10 months old when recordings started, but even Bartsch and Wellman couldn't be sure they had caught the earliest times when a child talked about mental states.

---

* Ages with full stops (i.e. 3.10) indicate years and months (i.e. 3 years and 10 months) and so are not decimal parts.

I wish, I want, I like, I think

Bartsch and Wellman were surprised to find children talking of desires from 18 months. Eve and Mark, both aged 18 months, were the first to use verbs like I want. But the talk soon got complex. Abe (aged 2 years and five months) heard his mother ask his father if he enjoyed the cranberry muffin. Abe added 'I wanna a cranberry muffin. I like them.' This was, in fact, a psychological explanation; Abe wants a cranberry muffin because he likes them.

A more complex conversation about motives was recorded when Ross, aged 2.6, was scratched by another boy.

Ross: *I want a Band Aid. The boy hurt me.*

Adult: *The boy hurt you. How did the boy hurt you?*

Ross: *The boy wanted to.*

Ross doesn't answer the 'how' question but he has no doubt that the boy intended to hurt him. Ross can attribute a mental state to his attacker.

Most 3-year-olds can talk about wishes and desires in a 'correct' way. Once they have mastered the basic vocabulary, more subtle expressions creep into the conversation usually by the age of 4. 'I hope' is an interesting verb. It's a very rare one for a 3-year-old to use and quite usual for a 4-year-old to use it.

Few parents will be surprised to learn children first talk about what they want and feel and only come later to discuss their thoughts and beliefs. In the Bartsch and Wellman study, about 1 in every 120 utterances concerned thoughts or beliefs while 1 in 40 concerned desires and wishes. They logged over 4,500 uses of these verbs. Every child had, by the age of 3 years and 5 months spoken of beliefs. The average age for first talking about beliefs was at 2 years 9 months.

But some children start to talk about thinking quite young as in the following exchange:

Adam (2.11): *I ... just thinking.*

Adult: *You're just thinking?*

Adam: *Yes.*

Adult: *What are you thinking about?*

Adam: *Thinking 'bout leaf.*

Slowly, children begin to use more exotic words such as wonder, expect, hope. As their vocabulary about feelings, beliefs and thoughts expands, they start to understand that other people are *other*, with other feelings and thoughts.

Bartsch and Wellman describe three different stages of the development of what philosophers call other minds.

Before the age of 2.0, children do not generally use the language of I wish and I desire or I want. They very rarely refer to thoughts and beliefs.

By the age of 3.0, children are much more likely to talk of thoughts.

By the age of 4.0, children are likely to talk of how other people think and feel and to use that as part of the explanation for behaviour. It seems 4-year-olds are well on the way to being able to see things from the perspective of others. They understand other people have other minds.

Wellman suggests children's increased psychological sophistication is due to 'a much wider range of exposure to social interaction. Children go to day care, they don't live in nuclear families, they engage more in pretend play and that has an effect.' He told me that children communicate with far more other people at younger ages than they did in the past. It grows them up.

False beliefs

If you understand other people have other minds, you know their point of view may be influenced by things which do not influence you. To test this, a particular kind of study has become almost standard – the *false belief study*.

The idea is simple. A child is shown two dolls – John and Sally. John hides an object behind a sofa. Sally is then taken out of the room. While she is gone, the object is hidden in a box. John has watched so he knows where the object now is. Not behind the sofa but in the box, a fact that Sally does not know. Logically, when she comes back, Sally should believe the object is still behind the sofa.

Children aged under 3 who watch this scenario do not understand that John knows something that Sally does not. John knows the object has been moved; but Sally does not know as she was out of the room when the move happened. If children under 3 are asked to say where Sally will look, they say she will search in the box. They cannot work out Sally has no reason to search in the box. The last she saw was the object being hidden behind the sofa – not in the box. Sensible Sally should look there.

Between 3 and 4 years of age, however, a dramatic change takes place. Most children start to get the picture. They see that from Sally's point of view, the sensible thing is to look for the object where she last saw it (i.e. behind the sofa); the 3-year-olds begin to 'see' into Sally's mind, if you like. When Sally left the room, the object was behind the sofa, so it is quite logical for her to seek it there. She has a logical false belief. One study (Joseph and Tager Flusberg, 1999) showed 94% of 4-year-olds understood the point.

Cutting and Dunn (1999) warn, however, that much of the research on pretending and false belief has been on middle-class and upper middle-class children; they have found a link between verbal ability and success on the false-belief task. Their warnings are particularly significant because recent work suggests a link between the inability to pretend play and autism.

If your child doesn't play – the mystery and misery of autism

Autism is a strange disease where the child speaks very little and is unable to communicate. For parents, it is very distressing. Niko Tinbergen, who won a Nobel Prize for studies of animal behaviour, had some autistic children in his wider family. That made him deeply interested in the topic. These children often seemed to behave like frightened animals and could be helped to make contact by coaxing them. Too much eye contact scared them, Tinbergen told me.

Nowadays, there is a better understanding of the symptoms of autism – and a steep steep rise also in the number of children who are affected by it and a milder form of the disease known as Asperger's syndrome. A review in the *Journal of the Royal Society of Medicine* in July 2000 lists 18 symptoms of autism. If a child shows just one or two, there is not that much cause for concern. But if the child shows 6 or more, then autism is a distinct possibility.

The criteria are written in jargon and I have tried to set them out more simply.

1   Abnormalities in social interaction in at least two of the following areas:

    (a)   poor eye-to-eye gaze, facial expression, body posture and gesture in social interaction;

    (b)   failure to develop peer relationships which involve some mutual interests, activities and emotions;

    (c)   failure to reciprocate in social and emotional situations or a deviant response to other people's emotions;

    (d)   no spontaneous attempt to share enjoyment – autistic children do not bring objects for other people to look at and play with, for example.

2 Abnormalities in communication:

    (a)   delay or lack of development of speech – autistic children sometimes compensate by using gesture or mime;

    (b)   relative failure to initiate or sustain conversation;

    (c)   stereotyped and repetitive use of language or idiosyncratic use of words;

    (d)   lack of spontaneous make believe or social initiative play.

3 Stereotyped behaviours:

    (a)   the child is preoccupied with one or more stereotyped patterns of interest;

    (b)   seemingly compulsive routines and rituals;

    (c)   repetitive motor mannerisms – the child flaps or twists fingers or hands or performs odd, complex body movements;

    (d)   the child is preoccupied with parts of objects or weird aspects of play objects – instead of playing with a teddy bear, the child is obsessed with the smell of the teddy or the feel of its fur.

Unfortunately, the discovery of the link between autism and inability to pretend play has not yet done much to promote a cure. Over the past 25 years, there have been hundreds of therapies recommended from swimming with dolphins to medication. The drug fenfluramine was much used in the 1980s in the United States and has now been largely withdrawn because of concerns about long-term damage. Secretenin injections are the latest miracle cure, but there is little proof of how well any of these therapies work.

If you are anxious about your child, go to the GP but also inform yourself by getting literature from groups like the National Autistic Society which provides good advice to parents.

The importance of pretending in normal development sometimes becomes evident to fathers at bath time and bedtime.

Getting away with laughter

Without anyone telling them, many children discover a very adult skill – that if you make someone laugh you can sometimes get away well not with murder but with quite a lot. I saw this in my own children when they were aged between 2 and 3 years. But I was far from the first to see it. The British psychologist James Sully (1912) noted a number of instances in which his boy aged 2.1 tried to get away with bad behaviour by laughing. The young Sully 'began to show himself a veritable rebel against parental authority.' He would sometimes hit his parents and 'follow up the sacrilege with a profane laugh.'

When Nicholas was 3 years 9 months and knew it was bedtime, he often devised games to delay. First, he would try a simple no. 'I won't', he said and laughed at me. Then he put his pyjama top the wrong way round quite on purpose. He laughed again, put his trousers on and span round like a top. 'Stop it,' I said. 'It's funny,' he insisted.

Nicholas was as capable of sacrilege as the young Sully. He also often laughed when he knew he was annoying or defying me by putting coins in his mouth, brushing his brother's toes with his toothbrush and other perverse, assertive acts of behaviour. Sometimes, he was really funny. I sometimes found it hard not to laugh when he brushed his brother's feet with the toothbrush – and he was convinced, in all his 3-year-old savvy, he would get away with it more easily if he made me laugh.

In games and pretending, children develop and show more and more personality.

Personality

Many fathers like jolly, outgoing children. But your child may not be like that. Withdrawn behaviour is not necessarily abnormal or autistic because we all have very different personalities as we saw in Chapter 3. Michael Apter who has developed Reversal Theory argues there are times and situations when some of us want calm and other times when we want excitement. We move between two states, he claims:

- telic state – where low arousal will be felt as calm and is pleasurable, while high arousal is felt as anxiety and unpleasant;
- paratelic state – where low arousal will be felt as boring and high arousal will be felt as fun.

But, Apter suggests, our biology also makes us either basically telic dominant or paratelic dominant. The telic dominant is serious-minded, ambitious and finds it hard to relax; the paratelic likes fun, play and buzz. One of Apter's most interesting insights is that our optimal level of arousal is related to our sense of playfulness. The playful, exuberant infant will become a paratelic individual who will, among other things, enjoy risk and cope well with it. The telic child will be more anxious and withdrawn for the rest of his life. Eysenck argued that you can see evidence of introversion in children from the age of 4.

Sex roles

As they play, children also learn to practice their gender roles. Boys are more aggressive and play with guns, girls with dolls. In play, children act out some of their conflicts and tensions. I am not a convinced Freudian myself but there is a curious point about play and the Oedipus complex which fathers need to ponder. According to Freud, small children are sexual creatures from birth, but after the oral, anal and genital phases, the child shuts down his sexuality. Around the age of 6, children go into what Freud called latency. They become a-sexual though they are often extremely interested in gender-appropriate behaviour. Boys play with soldiers, girls with dresses and make-up.

Freud argued latency was linked to resolving the Oedipus complex. One of the ways in which boys resolve this ancient Greek impediment is by identifying with the father. If dad is a hero and dad 'has' mum, and I am like dad, I somehow have mum too. The price I pay for the moment is to stop being a sexual being.

Freud never looked much at how children behave; instead, he studied what his patients remembered of their childhood. It seems plausible that the more time boys spend with their fathers, the easier identifying with dad will be. You will do with them the kinds of things you do. If, however, the more time you spend with your children, the more attached to you they are likely to become, where does that leave fathers and daughters? According to Freud, girls resolve their Electra complex by identifying with their mothers. Will a father who spends endless time with his 6–7-year-old daughter inadvertently reinforce her Electra complex? Especially, if the two of them spend much time alone? Will that girl find it harder for her to get over her crush on him? We don't know at present.

How children don't lie brilliantly

There are limits, thank God perhaps, on what children can manage. Flavell *et al.* (1997) find that pre-school children, even in California, find it hard to introspect. They get confused if asked to report their own feelings. And this confusion becomes very clear if we look at how children learn to lie.

The earliest lies are denials. The child is asked if he has hit his brother and says 'No'. Often children give themselves away by laughing nervously at the same time as they utter the lie. Young children do not like lying, according to Stephen Ceci, professor at Cornell University; so their body language often betrays them. Often, 3- and 4-year-olds place their hands in front of their mouth when telling lies. The symbolism is cute. The mouth has to be hidden because it is not speaking the truth.

By the time they are 5, most children do not do anything so obvious as cover their hands with their mouth when they are lying. They know adults would notice! But many children still cannot help giving more subtle non-verbal signals. They often look down at their feet and avoid all eye contact when they lie. If your child does this, he is in the jargon of non-verbal communication 'leaking' or showing 'leakage' because he or she isn't good at hiding the tension they feel.

I observed a textbook case of how 3-year-olds lie between David Carr Brown, Murielle and their 3-year-old Julian.

Box 5   A textbook case

'Did you spend the day with mummy,' David asked.

Julian smiled, clambered on his father's knee and clambered off again.

'And the goldfish died.'

'Were you very sad?'

'Doesn't matter,' Julian said. Then he clambered off his father's knee and disappeared into the bathroom. 'I'm having a pee,' he announced.

We then heard the water running. Two minutes later, Julian emerged from the bathroom with a small torch.

'What have you been doing with? It's wet', his mother asked.

Julian just smiled an angelic I-know-how-to-melt-my-parents smile.

'I want you to tell me,' his mother insisted.

'Tell your mother,' David added softly.

But Julian was fixed into angelic-smile mode. 'Nothing,' he finally said.

'It's wet,' his mother said, 'I don't mind what you do but I don't want you to lie.'

'Doesn't matter,' Julian said – just as with the dead goldfish.

At 3 and a half, Julian is trying to evade the answer. The parents know the child is lying; the child knows the parents think that but he wants to deflect attention away from that.

This little drama only stopped when his mother finally took him into the bathroom and asked what he had done.

'I wanted to see if it worked,' she returned shaking her head.

A psychologist teaches his daughter how to lie

Stephen Ceci claims children can get uncomfortable about lying even when the lie has no sinister implications – and he uses an anecdote to make the point. He had to take his 5-year-old daughter to hospital to see her mother who was having a routine operation. Ceci told his daughter to say she was 6-year-old if anyone asked because younger children were not allowed to visit the sick. They get in a lift and a nurse smiles at them. The nurse asks how old the little girl is:

'I'm five but he told me to say I was six,' says Ceci's daughter.

Ceci also set up situations in which his daughter was forced to lie to protect him. She had seen him steal some toys and he told her she must not get him into trouble. Film shows Ceci's daughter was uncomfortable, but she lied valiantly to protect her father. She twitched, she hesitated to speak, she tried to avoid eye contact, she showed 'leakage'. But she did not betray her dad. For Ceci the lesson is clear. Children lie much like adults do but, on the whole, they are less skilful about it.

Parents often pride themselves on knowing when their children are lying. Ceci's work suggests that this is not marvellous parental insight. What we are really doing is responding to the blatant cues children are giving us. We shouldn't flatter ourselves we always know what the little ones think.

Have fun with your kids

In the last 30 years, we have discovered a great deal about how child play, pretending and lying help children come to understand that other people exist. For fathers, the lessons are simple. When your children are little, play with them as much as you can. Rediscover the child in yourself. It will help you bond with your children.

Do as I say ...

Michael is always fidgeting, bouncing on the balls of his feet, running down the streets of north-west London. The top end of the Edgware Road is his territory. He's tense, intense, 17, streetwise. 'You don't want to look like a pussy on the streets. You're either a victim or you victimise,' he told me. He's an expert on local gangs and gang etiquette. Mugging women is not cool, but it is OK. Outside Kensal Rise tube, Michael showed me technique, the best stranglehold. It took him less than 10 seconds to grab them, grab their bag and run. 'I've only been caught once,' he smiles.

'My grandad used to look after me,' Michael told me. But then his grandad died. 'My mum she loves me ... but she's young at heart,' which means she has a succession of boyfriends. Michael hardly remembers his real father. Michael is intelligent and articulate but his school record was catastrophic. I met him at the offices of Young and Talented in Marylebone. He was taking a training course for disaffected teenagers who had excess attitude and zero qualifications, the unruly and unemployable. The course

leader had a soft spot for Michael but even he got exasperated. Michael would not turn up for interviews, would
walk out of jobs because he was bored, a catalogue of
missed opportunities and pissed employers.

Is Michael a delinquent? Yes. Is Michael a victim?
Yes, too. He's been failed by his parents, his schools,
the social services. London is littered with Michaels and
Michaels-to-be. While writing this book, I was involved
in a local drama on the way to the off-licence. It was 8
o'clock. My partner Julia and I decided to buy a bottle of
red wine.

A little Bengali boy was running down the road. He
looked about 3 years old. His yellow shirt was filthy; he
had no shoes or socks. He stopped at the traffic light. We
couldn't see any parent or adult in charge or an elder
brother or sister. I asked the boy if he was with his
mummy or daddy. 'Home,' he said and ran off at once.
He was fast, darted in between parked cars as if he were
trying to hide. He ran out into the street. Julia and I were
following now as were two other young men. We had no
idea where the boy lived. Everyone approached him
nicely. No one tried to grab him. But every time someone asked where his home was, he ran. He looked scared as
if we were hunting him.

Eventually, the boy went into a block of flats 300 yards
from the traffic lights where we had first met him. I went
to the first floor with one of the young men. At the end of a
long terrace, we found the boy's house. A tiny woman was
inside. She didn't seem remotely upset because he had run
away.

'Sorry,' she said.

She paid no attention to the little boy. She looked
completely out of it, either depressed or on drugs. We
reported it to social services, but this little boy will be
lucky if he doesn't turn into Michael.

In Britain, it is estimated that over 22,000 children do

not attend school every day for no good reason. A total of 100,000 children run away from home every year, a quarter being under 14, according to The Children's Society. The society also complains 11,000 children a year are sent to prison. The problems are international. In the Soviet Union, the authorities worry about the number of schoolchildren who take heroin and steal to maintain their habit. In America, the drug problem is even more extreme.

I am not about to peddle some magic formula for discipline. For the last 40 years, though psychologists have known the most effective ways of teaching discipline to most children. There are exceptions, of course. I'm not such a fanatic as to suggest there are perfect methods for all children. Nevertheless, motivation, punishment and reward are areas where psychology has made real advances.

Laws of psychology aren't quite like laws of chemistry and physics, however. If I observe how Saturn moves I have to be very odd to start getting mad at Saturn. If I imagine the rings of Saturn emit more carbon dioxide than usual to see if they can provoke me, I better head for the clinic for deranged astronomers. The laws of psychology are trickier since they involve human beings interacting with other human beings. One person can fine-tune her or his behaviour to needle you and that changes the situation. By the age of 4, many children understand enough about other people to be competent provokers.

I'm not about to go ESP on you, but most of us are also influenced by invisible presences – mainly our own parents, their attitudes to discipline and how we reacted, conscious and unconscious stuff. Being a good enough father requires, I want to suggest, a certain degree of honest introspection. The following questionnaire will give you some sense of your attitudes towards rules and discipline. As in the previous questionnaire, try to be honest. There are no right or wrong answers.

Box 6   Attitudes to discipline test

1 You discover your child has not gone to school. Which of the following is your most likely reaction:

   (a)   discuss with him why he or she is bunking off;
   (b)   discuss with the mother what to do about him;
   (c)   smack him the moment he comes home;
   (d)   wonder how often he has been doing this;
   (e)   blame yourself for it.

2 'The culture that things are no one's fault is weak. You have to be able to allocate blame.' Is this statement:

   (a)   right-wing liberal ignorance?
   (b)   untrue, sometimes no one is to blame?
   (c)   usually true (when things go wrong, you can find out who was responsible)?

3 You find your child is lying:

   (a)   do you lecture him or her on the need to tell the truth;
   (b)   tell him that if he ever does it again you will hit him;
   (c)   hit him;

(d) feel extremely upset that your child is behaving dishonestly;

(e) ask why he told that lie – and other lies.

3 When you think of your father, which of the following images comes to mind:

(a) a lion;
(b) a wolf;
(c) raging bull.

4 Which of the following statements most accurately reflects your feelings:

(a) no one can risk their children going out now;
(b) part of the job as a parent is to teach children about dangers so that they can take care of themselves;
(c) most children cope – and mine will too.

5 A recent criminal cases that attracted much publicity was Tony Martin who shot a 16-year-old burglar who was in his house. Which of the following do you think is right:

(a) he was entirely justified and should not be in jail;
(b) he was entitled to threaten the boy and call the police but not to shoot;
(c) he was wrong to take the law into his own hands.

6 The most important thing about your child for you is that:

(a) how well he or she does at school;
(b) how well he or she gets on with friends;
(c) how happy your child feels.

7 The European Court of Human Rights recent decisions expose parents who smack children to potential legal actions. Which of the following statements is closest to your reaction to that:

  (a) it was a sensible decision;
  (b) it is another sign of Brussels bureaucrats' unjustified meddling in our private lives;
  (c) in some societies banning smacking might work but not in Britain.

8 You catch your child stealing £2 from his mother's purse. Do you:

  (a) feel so outraged that you hit him;
  (b) remember that you stole things yourself when you were a kid;
  (c) discuss it with his mother.

9 You suspect your child is bullying some younger children. Do you:

  (a) hit him;
  (b) feel a bit proud he can stand up for himself;
  (c) tell him it has to stop and explain why;
  (d) discuss it with his mother and then confront him;
  (e) confront him and work out a punishment.

10 You suspect your child is bullying again. Do you:

  (a) tell his school;
  (b) try to cope with the situation by yourself in the family;
  (c) consult your doctor.

11 At a parent teacher evening, you discover your child has not been doing his work properly. Is your first reaction:

(a)   to tell him or her off for letting you down;
(b)   to feel ashamed you didn't know;
(c)   to explain firmly that being a lazy sod gets you nowhere in life;
(d)   to ask why;
(e)   to insist that from now on you will check it every night that homework has been done.

12 You catch your 13 year old rolling a joint. Do you:

(a)   report him to the police;
(b)   explain how you used to do it too;
(c)   warn him or her that getting hooked on cannabis is bad.

13 You find your 14 year old daughter has stayed out till 2 a.m. Do you:

(a)   feel worried because you have no idea who she was with;
(b)   talk to her mother about whether she has discussed contraception with her;
(c)   hit the roof;
(d)   say that she could have rung and that it wasn't fair to have you and her mother worried.

14 Your teenager goes on holiday with a party of friends. Do you expect:

(a)   a postcard;

(b) him or her to ring to say they got there safely;

(c) him or her to ring every day.

15 Your five-year-old is often rude to his granny. Do you:

(a) lose your temper because little children should be seen and not heard;

(b) think it cute that he's so sharp;

(c) take him aside and explain he's hurting his granny;

(d) smack him in front of her.

16 Your children quarrel all the time. Do you:

(a) try to understand why;

(b) ask yourself if either you or their mother are favouring one child;

(c) punish both of them;

(d) punish the child you think has started the quarrel.

The answers to the quiz are on p. 158.

Bad from birth

A surprising number of parents seem to believe that babies somehow know they are being bad and setting out to upset adults. I am not saying that babies can't drive you mad but the baby has no idea, no plan for what he is doing. So, don't blame the baby.

You can start talking of being naughty or bad behaviour somewhere around 18 months. Very often, the first acts of deliberate bad behaviour are simple refusals. I have often seen a toddler say 'no' and then laugh a very pleased laugh. Toddlers are not gorillas though great apes laugh when they triumph – and sometimes when the toddler who says no and laughs triumphantly we call him or her a little monkey.

As toddlers grow up, their naughtiness can become both irritating and more imaginative.

In the Greenwich playgroup, I made the following observation (the children were all aged between 3 and 4 years).

Sam, Giles and Robert (all 4 years old) are in the Wendy House out of sight. Sam: 'Shall we be dead and you be the doctor?' Sam and Giles lie down. Sam takes his pants off. Robert, the doctor, gets hold of the toy iron. He starts to iron Sam's bottom. Then he irons Sam's front. The children are completely quiet. Robert and Giles now also take their clothes off. Giles gets the iron and irons the others' bottoms.

The children become very quiet when they realise the grown-ups who run the nursery are outside. Four-year-olds are savvy enough to know they shouldn't be ironing each others' bums – and have sufficient insight into the adult mind to carry on without making too much noise.

The Wendy House was a privileged space where children could act out such semi-sexual behaviour. I would love to know whether psychologists who observed play in the 1920s and 1930s ever saw similar behaviour. I can find no sign of it either in Piaget, Valentine or Sully, but they may have felt that it was just not the kind of thing you would include in a serious scientific publication.

In the Greenwich nursery, when the head teacher Miss Sayer realised what was going on, she acted firmly but very calmly. She did not shout, she did not clout. She said that was quite enough of that and it was time to put clothes back on and come out of the Wendy House. She did not make a crisis out of it.

And that was the end of bottom ironing!

Miss Sayer, though a very proper spinster lady, showed no outrage, no moral panic. She did not behave as if she was in a battle. In *Happy Parents* (1970), however, Rudolf Dreikurs, a child psychotherapist, argued parents and children are engaged in a power struggle from the moment of birth. If parents let their children win, both are doomed to misery.

I have known times when being a parent feels like a power struggle with a small, wily enemy you love desperately. Mothers feel that even more at times as children take over their lives. Still, I think Dreikurs' view is extreme – and that, if you see yourself as being involved in a battle with your children, it will lead to needless tension and trouble.

Mastering the body

The first rules a child has to master is how to control bodily functions. The parents first job in terms of socialising the child is to toilet-train them.

Freud suggested toilet-training leaves its mark for the rest of its life. Some children do find toilet-training hard, though no one is clear how often that is because of physical problems.

Most children will be toilet-trained to sit on the pot between 18 months and 24 months. Many ask for that. Usually by the time they are 3, they will not need to wear a nappy except at night. Bed-wetting remains a problem for some children; though recent research suggests it does not, as once thought, lead to poor self-esteem.

Dr Sarah Redsell of the University of Leicester analysed
15 studies: she found that when children aged 5 and over
wet the bed it caused tension at home and those children
hated staying overnight with friends, scared they'd have
an accident.

Masturbation

Many parents also find it hard to cope with any sign of
sexuality in small children. It is perfectly normal, in fact,
for toddlers to touch and play with their genitals. A
century ago, Freud fought to get his liberal views accepted. He had been trained at a time when many psychiatrists spoke of masturbation leading to madness. He
had never seen any real evidence for that; he insisted that
childhood sexuality was normal, a lesson society still often
struggles with. One of Freud's students, the analyst W.
Stekel put it clearly 'the damning of the auto erotic activity frequently causes the child to wet himself, to stammer
and to exhibit various symptoms of defective behaviour,
symptoms that are but evidence of internal revolt.' In
other words, not masturbating leads to madness!

Freud's theories had a powerful influence on 1920
experts like Bertrand Russell, John B. Watson himself
and A. S. Neill who was specially passionate on the
subject of masturbation. Freud also argued many little
boys were terrified of being castrated every time they
touched themselves. Mummy or nanny or daddy threatened that if he didn't stop doing that, it would be cut off.
This wasn't just a conscious fear. The child associated
touching its genitals with sexual power. In the fury and
chaos of the Oedipus complex, the child knew unconsciously he should not have sexual power. So, unconsciously, the boy felt he deserved to be castrated.

If a small child masturbates, do not lose your cool. It is entirely normal and there is no evidence that it will do any damage.

By the age of 4–5 years most children have learned not to be touching themselves in public. If your child still does so, talk to them about why they should not. Do not hit them. Do not threaten to cut their willy off. What you can do, however, is explain that there are certain things you do not do when other people are there and are watching.

Individual family

Every family will have its own dos and don'ts. Some children will conform easily; they want their parents' approval. Others will be more difficult, more rebellious. There are personality differences. Extrovert children are harder to discipline, according to Eysenck, because they enjoy the risky and dangerous.

Teenagers, as we shall see, often do provoke their parents. They refuse to X because Mum or Dad insists they do X. But this is much less the case with younger children. If your relationship with your small children starts to feel like a power struggle, you need to analyse what you are doing very carefully.

Usually, when relationships between adults break down, we blame the other – unreasonable cow, pathetic bastard – but most of us know it takes two to fight. With a child, you as the adult are bigger, wiser, more experienced and control the pocket money.

I am sorry to sound preachy but you have to ask: What are you doing to make it worse? What are you doing to create the tensions?

The pressure on parents

One reason why parents feel under pressure is that society expects them to control their children. And the most eminent can feel that. When Euan Blair, the son of the Prime Minister, was found drunk in Leicester Square, his parents were made to feel they failed. For days, the tabloids harped on Euan Blair's 'problem'. Being drunk in Leicester Square is not that serious, but the combination of sneering and disapproval in the tabloids was unpleasant. How many parents have never had to deal with such a crisis?

Sometimes, a child doesn't just behave badly but commits serious crimes. And that can drive fathers deep into guilt.

The father of the serial killer Jeffrey Dahlmer wrote a memoir in which he explained what had gone wrong. Less extreme, John McVicar, the armed robber who was Britain's Public Enemy No. 1 in the 1970s and then did a sociology degree while in prison, also had to face a parenting problem. After leaving prison, he told me he was very sad that his son had followed in his first footsteps. In an open letter in the *Spectator*, McVicar pleaded with his son to learn from his mistakes. He suspected his son was trying to prove he was harder than his old man, his old man who had wimped out to become a sociologist. McVicar was both sad and angry that he had not persuaded his son that crime was a waste of talent.

Psychologists like Lawrence Kohlberg, who have studied the moral development of children, suggest that children grasp the concept of rules well before they are 6 but they have no real moral sense. By the age of 9, however, normal children have grasped most basic social rules and do know right from wrong. Kohlberg (1984) was not advising parents but it follows from his research that the more parents, explain why something is right or wrong the more likely children are to accept society's rules. But, today, few parents have the unquestioning moral compass the Victorians had.

In a time of confusion, it is hard to know exactly what behaviour to expect from children (Box 7).

Box 7   The good enough father wants to have a good enough child

The good enough child will usually behave appropriately in the following situations.

Reasonable behaviours by the age of 2–3 years:

- should be toilet-trained;
- should go to bed without fuss except in exceptional circumstances;
- will not run away or wander away from parents;
- will not run into the road;
- will not hit other children;
- will not have frequent temper tantrums.
- will be friendly to other children and adults.

Unreasonable behaviours by age of 2:

- none really.

It is reasonable to expect a 7-year-old will have the discipline:

- to go to school every day;
- to co-operate with his brothers and sisters;

- to listen if you explain what he is doing that is naughty;
- not to steal;
- not to put himself in danger stupidly by lighting fires or rushing out into the road;
- not to masturbate in public;
- not to lie very much … be real, no human being never lies;
- not to bully other children;
- will tell you if there are troubles with any of the above;
- will tell you if he or she is having problems at school or with other children.

Unreasonable behaviours by the age of 7:

- violence;
- swearing;
- running away, all fairly extreme manifestations of problems not just with the child but in the family.

The question of what children understand about right and wrong is only part of discipline. Your feelings as a father have a long history and it's useful to think back to your own childhood and to how you reacted to your parents.

BP shares are down – thwack …

My father had his flash points. Any son of his had to do well at school. The fate of oil shares also had a profound influence on his mood. If my reports were bad and BP was down, I was in for the high jump.

The usual domestics made it worse. He and my mother were not happy. If she started to nag him, either about buying a new sofa, or about whether he had been unfaithful again – if he had been caught with the secretaries, a new sofa was the minimum compensation – he was more likely to get angry and thump me. He was not fundamentally a violent man and he had certainly read Montaigne's views on not beating children. But that did not help him control his temper. I found his rages frightening. Till I was 11 or 12, I knew I had to be careful if he was in one of those moods. My experience was not exceptional. Blendis (1988) found many men remembered their fathers as being highly authoritarian.

The fact that my father smacked me had its impact. Aileen objected to smacking profoundly, but there were a few times when I did hit our children. I never felt very guilty about it partly I think because I never lost control. I never hit and kept on hitting. My father had sometimes been so angry, so red in the face with fury, he seemed unable to stop himself. He did collect himself after a few blows, but I was always scared he might not. He slapped hard but it wasn't just the pain, he was unpredictable. His fury was as much about the way he felt as about what I had done. I tried to be more predictable. I hope I don't fool myself when I say that when I smacked my children, I was always trying to make a point. I immediately explained why whatever he had done was dangerous or wrong. I cooled it.

Despite his outbursts of violence, my father was a good model in one way. He never made nasty fun of me or ridiculed me. Once when I was 16, he took me on a business trip to Nice. With true teenage pompousness, I lectured him and his associates on how to handle a tricky insurance deal.

My father said calmly, 'I'm glad we heard what you have to say and now we must analyse it from a different point of view.' He did not laugh at my pumped up persona, the teen insurance guru.

The holy slipper and the holy cane

We came to live in Britain when I was 8 and I was educated in a school system where beating children was normal. My prep school had been set up by a descendant of William Gladstone. Gladstone had fought against persecution in Eastern Europe; his followers practised it in Eaton Square.

The Latin master beat you with a small, wooden bat if you got your declensions wrong; another master flicked lighted matches at you if you misbehaved or were stupid about fractions. His aim was excellent and we were frightened he'd set fire to our hair. The match usually fizzled out in flight. One day, his smile suggested, he would succeed in setting fire to a boy – and the tyke would deserve it. Both teachers had been scarred by World War II and one apparently had marital difficulties. I was not living through an unusual hell, however. John Mortimer, in his autobiographical play *Voyage round My Father* (1970), describes going to a prep school where veterans of the 1914 war hurled various objects at pupils. Shell shock, battle trauma and caning in British schools, a good subject for a PhD thesis!

When my son Nicholas went to school at a rather more modest private school called Riverston in the 1970s, children there lived in fear of 'the slipper'. Mr Lewis, the owner of the school and of slipper, believed the application of the slipper 'when it was deserved' only benefited the child. It taught him the rules of the school and of life.

These *Beat-the-Boys* tales are still relevant in Britain at the start of the 21st century. The British associate the heyday of empire with public schools where corporal punishment was part of the culture. If the battle of Waterloo was won on the playing fields of Eton, it was won by officers who (unlike Napoleon) had had the inestimable advantage of being flogged by their teachers and fellow pupils.

More than any other European country, Britain accepts that parents have a right to punish children physically. Brilliant critiques, such as Lindsay Anderson's great film *If* and a number of George Orwell's essays, do not stop today's tabloids moaning that the bureaucrats of Brussels have robbed British boys and girls of their birthright – to be beaten.

A history of the cane and carrot

The psychologists who first tried to work out effective programmes of discipline were known as behaviourists. Behaviourism claimed we are all conditioned, or shaped, by the way we are punished and rewarded. The two most influential behaviourists of the 20th century were John B. Watson (1878–1958) and B. F. Skinner (1904–1990). Both men were committed to using psychology to help people.

I interviewed Skinner twice in the 1970s. He was upset by what he saw as deliberate, almost malicious attempts to paint him as a punishment-crazed control freak. Skinner found that you could shape the behaviour of criminals like rats and pigeons. If a rat started to run down a maze, you would reward it with a pellet of food and, so lead it on till it explored the whole maze. Once you had shaped the behaviour, the most effective rewards were intermittent. A rat being trained to press a lever would be rewarded with sugar, say 5 times in 100. The lesson the rat learned was to keep on pressing. Using a similar schedule of reinforcement, Skinner even taught pigeons to play ping-pong.

Skinner worked in institutions like prisons, mental hospitals and children's homes. He found so-called 'token' economies were the most effective in shaping be-haviour. In a token economy system, you are rewarded for good behaviour and the rewards are set down in advance. For example, you get 2 points if you make your bed in the morning and 5 points if you help clear up breakfast. You lose points for bad behaviour; again there is a tariff. Hitting someone would lose you 10 points. Points buy privileges like an evening out and the money to buy a pizza.

In a token-economy system, however, you are never punished physically or ridiculed.

Skinner argued the most effective way to discipline a child is to pick out desirable behaviours and reinforce them with points, with praise and with attention. Rewards worked better than punishments. Skinner felt so strongly he wrote a novel, *Walden Two*, about a utopian community where children were rewarded for good, co-operative behaviour. Bad behaviour led to with-drawal of privileges.

Skinner was puzzled that people did not want to hear what he was saying. It was claimed he and his wife had brought up their daughter in a Skinner box which meted out punishments to her. That was a total lie, he told me. He was also furious when Stanley Kubrick's *A Clockwork Orange* was released and the press claimed the techniques of punishment used on the young thug were ones Skinner advocated. In the film, electrodes were implanted in the brain so that every time the hero had an antisocial thought he was shocked. He soon learned to suppress evil antisocial thoughts.

The general principles Skinner and Watson developed are not hard to set out:

1 Physically punishing children rarely works and has potentially serious neurotic side effects.

2 It is better to get a child to behave well by rewarding him or her for positive behaviour than by punishing them for bad behaviour.

3 The most useful form of punishment is often to withhold attention and affection.

4 Always explain to a child in terms she or he can understand why what they have done is wrong. This need not mean getting involved in an argument, but it does mean achieving a certain distance and not getting sucked into too much drama.

Skinner and Watson wrote decades ago, however, but it is a measure of their failure to convince that America today locks up more children per 100,000 of the population than any other democratic country. Britain also incarcerates more children than any other European country, often in appalling conditions. Sir David Ramsbotham, then the Inspector of Prisons, repeatedly complained about the dreadful facilities for young prisoners – and little was done. Our cultures are punitive even though we know punishment doesn't work. If politicians will not learn the lessons, it seems hardly fair to blame fathers if they find it hard to follow the best scientific advice. But fathers need to face some facts.

The European Court of Human Rights is taking an increasingly tough line against smacking. In 1990, the case of *A v UK* concerned the severe beating of a 9-year-old by his stepfather. The issue of child abuse was very much in the air and the severity of the beatings meant that the stepfather got relatively little support from the British media. The European Court of Human Rights did not go so far as to say that corporal punishment amounts to a violation of Article 3 of the convention on the rights of the child. It ruled, however, that, as children are vulnerable, they are entitled not to have their personal integrity violated. The Court held that the stepfather had breached Article 3. Since the Court has ruled children are vulnerable, that decision has made it much harder for anyone to justify hitting their children.

If you feel you can only control your child by hitting them, ponder. In some European countries like Sweden and Holland, it is illegal to smack children. Usually, when judges sit, you know they have no experience of what they are trying. They have not really been tempted to rob a bank. Most of the judges on the European Court are parents and presumably have some idea of how mad children can drive you.

In Britain, smacking is not illegal. If you feel it is your parental right to smack, remember some safety basics. Babies should certainly never be smacked. If you want to use a smack to teach a lesson, you have to (1) stay in control and (2) be able to explain to the child precisely why you have smacked him or her. You can't hope to do that before the child understands what you are saying. The only reason to smack a child is to make a very serious point very forcefully. Smacking is not a release of your tensions.

Psychologists now think they can see three different styles of discipline.

Styles of discipline

Strong discipline

The child needs to be punished if she or he misbehaves. No one is recommending being cruel to children, but if they don't listen the first time, then the only way we will get through is by giving them a good smack. Parents who practise strong discipline often care about their children a great deal, but they tend to see them as being unable to listen to reason. Children have to be trained like animals.

Emotional discipline

Parents who believe in this approach do not exclude smacking a child, but that will be seen as very much a last resort. The child can be taught, if you praise them

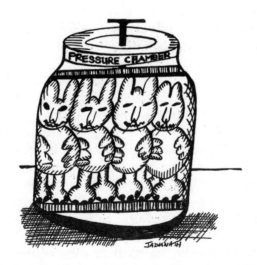

Under pressure – avoid doing this to your kids

when they are good and tell them off when they are bad. But telling them off also includes emotional withdrawal and, very often, making the child feel bad about himself or herself because they have let their parents down.

Laissez-faire

This school believes that we must trust in the spirit of the child. Perhaps the most dramatic example of this are free schools like A. S. Neill's Summerhill. Neill believed children should not be forced to attend classes they did not want to. Punishment was anathema to him. Neill believed children were by nature co-operative; he also believed that they wanted to learn. When adults and parents tried to impose their will on the child, it crushed the spirit of the child.

Baumrind (1988) gives a similar analysis of styles of discipline which she called *authoritarian, authoritative* and *permissive*. The authoritarian father believes in clear rules, no arguments or explanations and the right to smack a child; the authoritative father is clear about rules but is willing to explain and discuss. He is also nearly always warm to the child. The permissive father ignores boundaries and trusts in the child.

The use of authoritative parenting

Baumrind looked at the effects of the three different styles using a variety of methods. She visited the home, talked to fathers, mothers and the children. She argued authoritative parents are warm, loving, responsive and supportive.

They respect their child's independence, their point of view and their personality. They talk to the children about what they like and what interests them. When they stop the children doing something, they don't just issue an edict but they explain their reasons. At the same time, they demand mature behaviour, but mature behaviour does not always mean doing the conventional thing.

Baumrind compared the same children before they went to school and when they were 9-years-old. She asked teachers to rate their behaviour. She found that 9-year-olds who had been brought up authoritatively were more competent intellectually and socially. They were better at making plans. They were also more friendly and co-operative than the children of authoritarian or permissive parents.

For both boys and girls, this style of parenting and discipline worked. Being authoritative does not mean showing no feelings. Zahn Wexler *et al.* (1979) found that where mothers explained and were emotional, it left a lasting impact. Typical interventions were 'look what you did. Don't you see you hurt Amy?' This worked much better than either hitting Amy or just telling her to stop. This style is, of course, the very opposite of in-difference. The parent shows he, or she, cares because he or she is emotional, emotional but controlled – and con-trolled enough to explain what a child has done wrong immediately.

All this work makes it clear what the most effective forms of discipline are – and we can see the development from the ideas of Watson and Skinner. Praise, explain, discuss, punish by sowing disapproval rather than smack-ing. The trouble is that not all parents will find these attitudes congenial. For some, they will go directly against the grain of their personality. For some parents it does feel like a battle with the children. It is also a question of how you cope with your own feelings, particularly if they seem to be getting the better of you and you are not in emotional control. That can be frightening. The scenario in Box 8 is one that some fathers will recognise:

Box 8   Benny misbehaves

I can't stand it when he misbehaves.
I must be patient. I know I'm in a bad mood. I had a row at work with my boss.
I just want Benny to stop crying about wanting Beanie Babies.
I tell him to shut up.
'Beanie Babies,' he cries.
I've had it.
I slap Benny – hard.
If he'd shut up, as I told him to, I wouldn't have had to hit the little bastard.
Benny screams.
I hate Benny screaming.
I keep hitting Benny.
I feel better, I feel exhausted.
Benny looks hurt.
I wrap my arms to comfort Benny.
Benny runs away.
I know that I'm to blame.
But he shouldn't run away.
I was trying to say sorry.
I was trying to show love.

> *The little bastard ran away.*
> *That's no way to treat his father.*
>
> In this do you recognise nothing at all? You are
> never like that. Do you never lose control?

Bullying

A good example of a muddled approach to discipline is to
be found in the *Parents & School* magazine issued by
the Department of Education and Employment. A large
article is devoted to how to help your child if he or she is
being bullied. About a hundred words are devoted to the
equally serious problem of what to do if it is your child
who is the bully.

The Department of Education takes a rather feeble
line. It recommends that you:

- find out exactly what sort of bullying they've been
  involved in;
- ask whether anything is bothering them;
- reassure them you don't love them less but tell them
  you don't like their behaviour.

The Department does not tell parents they should tell the
child their bullying has to stop. It does not suggest
parents ask tough but necessary questions – like is their
child not just bullying but extorting money from weaker
children, a frequent problem. It does not explain why
bullying is wrong and it is silent on the question of
what parents tell the school. Michael Crick in his excellent biography of Jeffrey Archer claims, for example, that
Archer was bullied at school and that this contributed to

his problems. Many parents will not want to betray their children. I hope I would have had the courage to tell my sons' school if I suspected them of bullying.

Part of the problem is that we do find it hard to talk seriously to children about serious things. This failure is linked to a rather wider malaise uncovered by Stephen Ceci who is not just an expert on lying but also on how reliable children are as witnesses. By the end of the 1980s, he was recognised as a leading researcher on child memories when he was faced with an unexpected challenge.

How to question children

One day, Ceci took a disturbing phone call from a judge. A woman's body had been found concreted below her living room. Her sister claimed she had been killed by her husband. The victim's son was the key witness. The prosecution claimed the child recalled that, when he was 4, he had seen his father hitting his mother with a baseball bat. 'The judge wanted to know if he could believe a child's memories of such an event,' Ceci told me. Ceci had spent years researching children's memories, but he had focused on how children recall lists on nonsense syllables such as CAX, TIR and WEG. (This is a classic subject in psychology; the first experiments were done in 1885.) 'I was clueless,' he told me.

Ceci decided to research how children remember events in real life, events which have some emotional pull. It has taught him both that children have surprisingly good memories but also that the way adults, including parents, ask them questions often makes them confused. 'After 10 years, I'm struck by how well children, as young as 3, remember ordinary events, 'Ceci said.

A total of 95% can describe accurately an event from 3 months previously. But it is not easy to get those memories out. 'The problem is the adults who have access to children's memories,' Ceci said.

When allegations of abuse are made, children have to talk to social workers, police, lawyers, psychologists. Young children don't like to talk about embarrassing events – and they often clam up. Many interviewers don't know how to respond to that silence. The right technique is not to rush but to wait and gently prompt the child. Instead, many interviewers bombard the child with questions. Parents are often exasperated when children will not reply to questions, and so they start to bully their children. In social-work situations, Ceci found, interviewers often ask leading questions and the phrasing of these questions influences not just what children say but what they start to believe. 'Suggestive' questions can make a child create 'false beliefs'.

Ceci devised a series of experiments where children aged 3, 4 and 6 years had an unexpected visitor to their classroom, Sam Stone. He walked in, said something about the book being read to the class, did absolutely nothing and then left, having spent perhaps 2 minutes in the classroom. Normally, children remembered Sam coming into the room and said, accurately, that nothing more happened.

'But if you start to seed things,' Ceci said, 'you can make children believe something very different happened.' Some children were told that Sam was clumsy and often broke things; others were questioned in ways which suggested there had been trouble when Sam was in class. The effect was dramatic. Most children (72%) then embroidered the story and quite a few added details of Sam's destructive behaviour. But there had been no destructive behaviour, of course. If children are questioned in a way that 'seeds', they can easily start to believe things that did not happen did happen. Ceci has found 35% of 6-year-olds can develop such false beliefs.

The mousetrap but not by Agatha Christie

Ceci showed me a dramatic video which illustrates his warnings. In this video, a 5-year-old boy was asked about an incident when he had gone into the basement of his home and found a mouse. There was no mouse in reality, but the questions also probed how the boy's finger had been caught in the mousetrap. The boy was then asked how he felt when was taken to hospital. The story was a lie from beginning to end but, after a few weeks of questioning, the 5-year-old had obviously come to believe there was a mouse and that he had got his finger caught in the mousetrap.

The boy said he had been taken to the hospital because his finger hurt so much and explained why. This slightly fairy-tale study shows how easy it is for well-meaning social workers and police officers to prompt children so they remember incidents of child abuse which never happened.

Studying police investigations, Ceci found some farcical mix-ups. For example, a woman called the police when her 3-year-old daughter said that 'daddy put his pee-pee in my pee-pee.' The truth turned out to have nothing to do with abuse. The girl had gone to toilet, peed and not flushed; 'daddy' had gone to the bathroom later, peed and, just as the girl said, put his pee-pee into her pee-pee.

Ceci's technique offers real lessons — both if you think your child is causing trouble like bullying and also if you think your child needs help. I know from experience that it is not always easy to read the signals.

Not picking up the clues children give

Bad listening can lead to bad guild. When our boys were 10 and 6, Aileen and I hired on ultra-respectable young women to look after them when they got back from school. The girl was the daughter of a couple from the local Quaker meeting. That seemed almost a guarantee that she was responsible and kind. We did not notice that our younger son was getting withdrawn.

After a number of months, Nicholas finally plucked up the courage to tell us the 'baby sitter' was spiteful and sometimes violent to our younger son. She screamed at him for no good reason and, sometimes, even hit him. We had no idea. As we were very self-absorbed at the time, we did not talk to the children enough about what was happening. When we found out, we sacked her at once but it had been going on for too long. If you do use a nanny or a childminder, get serious references and be very vigilant. We had totally failed to learn how to give our children the chance to explain what was wrong.

Lessons for fathers

Be prepared to listen. Give your child time. If you think your child has done something wrong, ask open-ended questions such as 'What did you do then ...' rather than 'Did you or did you not steal Willy's truck?'. Above all, do not get flustered yourself when the child does not reply quickly. These techniques may be specially relevant in stepfamilies.

I want to end this chapter by offering some basic advice on how to manage anger because fathers are sometimes overwhelmed by it.

Basic anger management

Work does affect our moods. A study of stock-market dealers, *Stress in the Dealing Room* (1993), found many dealers worked in highly pressured City jobs and worried that they brought all their stress back home. They drank too much and their tempers were short. If something had gone wrong at work that day, their wives and children suffered. Dealers are not exceptional. Pilots, train drivers, social workers, doctors, middle managers, lawyers and the unemployed have all reported they suffer from high levels of stress. So do motorists. Men who feel stressed admit they lose their temper more easily.

Studies of child abuse repeatedly find significant numbers of children have been victims of serious violence. In the majority of cases of physical and sexual abuse, the father or stepfather is the perpetrator. In this section, I just want to deal with physical abuse. It is very hard to get people to talk honestly about what drives them to it. There is no doubt that many men who hit their children were themselves brought up in households where they were often clouted and belted. Some men who survive such a childhood feel they have every right to lord brute physical power over their children. Many other men with the same background may bully and hit their children, but feel uneasy about doing it.

No one will get their temper and violence under control if they don't recognise what they are doing is wrong. A first step is to look a drinking patterns. Alcohol always makes the problem worse; studies in

Britain and Australia both show 80% of the cases of domestic violence involve drink. A drunken father is a dangerous father (Elliott, 1995).

If you do often feel violent and enraged, you need help. In an ideal world, seek counselling help. Probably the best qualified organisations are those that specifically deal with child abuse like Child Line and the NSPCC.

Many men resist counselling, however, They promise that it won't happen again, that they will get their temper under control by sheer will power. That can happen, but it is rare. Violent men need help and they hate the fact, because needing help makes them feel helpless. It doesn't mean that at all. It is trying to solve a desperate problem.

One technique may help stop anger from getting out of control. Try to isolate exactly what triggers the desire to hit your child. Specific triggers some fathers report that make them tense and angry include:

- the sound of the baby crying;
- persistent whining;
- throwing food or objects and making a mess;
- demands for food;
- demands for attention;
- the mother fussing over the child;
- the mother criticising you;
- feeling that the child will not stop, the child is out of control;
- feeling that if you hit the child then it will stop;
- a child wetting or soiling.

A baby or a young child is helpless, defenceless and cannot threaten you. You are seeing things perversely if you are being sucked into a power struggle with a creature who weighs less than 3 stone. Crying, whining, running away are the only weapons the child has – and, nearly always, what the child is doing is either expressing pain or trying to get your attention.

Violent men need professional counselling but the following techniques are worth trying too.

Some fathers report it has helped them to do some relaxation and deep-breathing training. They use this when their child screams; they learn not to get agitated, not to feel they have to do something. They breathe, they relax, they try to assess the situation and work out why the child is crying.

And that reframing makes them less likely to hit out almost automatically.

Dealing with domestic violence is difficult – and even more so for your family than for you. Men have to face up to the problem. If you don't, your family will be hurt psychologically as well as physically. At the end of the book, I list organisations which can offer specific help. But it is not the case that men can't change.

Abraham broke his daughter's arm when she was in her teens. He is a professional man and he had a long history of being violent to his wife and children. He was never quite sure what made him lose his temper. For years, he refused to seek help; when his wife suggested he needed therapy it would make him angrier. Their neighbours had no idea what was going on for years. When they found out, they did nothing to protect the children because they felt too embarrassed. Eventually, after inflicting a nasty beating on one daughter, Abraham agreed to seek counselling. The counselling did not go well. Abraham came out of it with a justification. He now suspected he became violent because his wife wound him up, as his mother had wound him up years ago. In the past, Abraham was always very ashamed after he lost his temper. Now, he could explain his lack of control in super psychobabble.

Some months later, Abraham broke his daughter's arm. Usually, his attacks had left his wife and children bruised. This was the worst ever. His daughter was then in her teens. She was furious and said she would not speak to him again till he tried to sort it out. She had the courage to draw the line. Abraham loved his family. This time he found a counsellor who did not just analyse but also gave him alternative ways of coping. The counsellor repeated that violence simply was unacceptable. Abraham did not find it easy to stop his violent behaviour. He left home for a time but eventually he felt he would lose everything if he did not make every effort to change. So he didn't give up.

In Abraham's case, counselling eventually did work. He and his family are reunited and he is a proud grand-father. 'He finds his grandchildren easier than he did his children,' his wife said.

All parents feel they fail sometimes with discipline. Do not beat yourself up over that. You cannot be the perfect disciplinarian any more than you can be the perfect father. But the good enough father lays down boundaries, does not lose his cool and is always ready to explain why something is wrong. Perhaps the only rule is to never to say 'just do as I say'. Well, not never but as rarely as you can.

Answers to quiz on p. 128

1 a. *L*   b. *L*   c. *A*   d. *N*   e. *N*

2 a. *A*   b. *L*   c. *S*

3 a. *S*   b. *N*   c. *A*

4 a. *A*   b. *L*   c. *L*

5 a. *A*   b. *S*   c. *L*

6 a. *A*   b. *L*   c. *L*

7 a. **L**   b. **A**   c. **S**

8 a. **A**   b. **L**   c. **S**

9 a. **A**   b. **A**   c. **L**   d. **S**   e. **S**

10 a. **S**   b. **L**   c. **N**

11 a. **A**   b. **N**   c. **S**   d. **L**   e. **S**

12 a. **A**   b. **L**   c. **S**

13 a. **N**   b. **L**   c. **A**   d. **S**

14 a. **L**   b. **S**   c. **N**

15 a. **A**   b. **L**   c. **S**   d. **A**

16 a. **L**   b. **N**   c. **A**
      d. score both an **A** and **S**

The aim of the test is judge whether you tend to be authoritarian and punitive (**A**), liberal and *laissez-faire* (**L**), and stable (**S**) or neurotic (**N**).

Total possible **A** score 15. Below 5, you are not very authoritarian. About 9, your first reactions are often highly authoritarian and this may be a style you need to think about changing.

Total possible **L** score 15. Below 5, you are not very *laissez-faire*. Above 9, you need to think about whether you are trying to be too liberal perhaps.

Total possible **S** score 13. Relatively stable but not too relaxed parents will score 6–8 here. If you score under 5, you tend to be either authoritarian or liberal.

The **N** score is a measure of anxiety as a parent. Total possible score 6. If you get above 3 your first reaction is often to worry and, sometimes rightly sometimes wrongly, to blame yourself. Ask yourself why.

6

School and the mind

In 1690, the philosopher John Locke advised his friend
Edward Clark and his wife on how to give their young
children the best possible education. Japan, said Locke,
but he wasn't referring to their cramming. The Clarks
should talk to their children as if they were travellers
who had just landed from Japan. To a child, everything
would seem new and strange.

Locke also suggested a clever game for teaching the
alphabet. The child sat with his parents, a book and cakes
baked in the shape of letters. When the child recognised a
letter he could eat it. The game was, in fact, a Jewish
tradition used since the Middle Ages. Parents and rabbis
were teaching children that learning is sweet. Eat your
letters worked brilliantly. Most Jewish children, girls as
well as boys, knew how to read and write when the Christian world was still largely illiterate. It has been suggested
this contributed to making Jews intellectual; three of the
thinkers who shaped the modern world – Marx, Freud,
Einstein – were Jews, though hardly Orthodox ones.

The No. 15 bus and good enough fathering

Fathers do often teach their sons. I was reminded of this on top of a No. 15 bus going in to the West End. My fellow passengers included an American man in his 40s and his 5-year-old son. The boy was standing up. The father had an arm close, ready to pat his son and protect him. The boy looked ahead, curious. Their conversation went like this:

Boy: *Dad what do those letters spell A H E A D?*

Dad: *Ahead. They put it there for cars.*

The bus conductor came to the top deck and asked if everyone had tickets or a pass:

Boy: *Do I have to unfold my ticket?*

Dad: *No, he's seen your ticket.*

Boy: *You sure, Dad?*

The boy fidgets in his pocket, shows his Dad the ticket, obviously wants to show that he is competent enough to show the conductor his ticket:

Dad: *You don't need to. He knows he sold us tickets.*

Boy: *What's the name of that building?*

Dad: *St Paul's Cathedral.*

For the first time, now Dad asks a question:

Dad: *Is it to the left or right?*

Boy: *To the left.*

Dad: *Think again.*

The boy smiles. His father obviously asks trick questions sometimes:

Boy: *To the left.*

Dad: *It's to the right. Did you leave your brain at home?*

Boy: *[laughs] I didn't leave my brain at home.*

Five minutes of good enough fathering and, without making a display, father helped his son learn about St Pauls, the etiquette of ticket collection and where left and right are.

Many children, however, do leave their brains at home when they go to school. Educational systems often crush natural curiosity. Children have to learn the obscure, the irrelevant and the over-academic – and in Britain these are the privileged who go to public schools.

From the ages of 14 to 16, I, the Jew David Cohen, could explain the different views on transubstantiation held between 1520 and 1550 by the Pope (the blood and wine do really change into the body of Christ), by Luther (it's largely symbolic, not chemical magic), by Satanic Calvin (it's totally symbolic and it's only the anti-christian Pope who thinks otherwise), and by minor gurus such as

Zwingli, Munster and Melanchthon. I never told the rabbi of my expertise. I was embarassed that Christian theological arguments came easily to me.

When we lived in Lewisham, we found the state system so bad I persuaded Aileen our children should go to public school as I had done. In the 1980s, our children spent years learning about containers. Containers travelled the globe – geography; containers carried goods – economics; today, illegal asylum seekers stow away in containers so they could also be politics and sociology.

The host or the haulage – just which can we expect a teenager to care more about?

Though the Blair government is committed to education, education, education, in many parts of Britain comprehensive education is still not working well. There are many reasons for this. Middle-class parents buy out of the state system. State schools often do not have good facilities. They are less ambitious for children. Some educationalists even blame Piaget's theories, claiming that he argued children should not be made to learn things by rote and not be taught formally how to read, write or do arithmetic.

Part of the drive to improve standards is to make parents and schools work together. The Department of Education and Employment encourages schools to produce a home–school agreement which outlines the duties of parents. Parents promise to get the children to school regularly, to let the school know of problems which might affect the child, to support doing homework and to attend parents' evenings. Just what parents can do if they disagree with this contract is not clear though.

The Department's magazine, *Parents & Schools* (free at supermarkets), is full of hot tips. The tone is jolly and a little hectoring. Top stories include 'Get Kids Bananas about Maths' and 'How to Make them Happy Mondays', happy so that kids go to school. It speaks of meetings which 'offer the parents a chance to meet the teacher in a non threatening way.' Nowhere does the Department admit schools and parents often have problems with each other. It's rosy and sunny time. Happy parents and efficient schools work in partnership to produce happy, able children. The magazine even has a quiz which asks mum and dad 'have you done your homework about homework?'

I have to reproduce one of its questions ...

Your child wants to know where Ulan Bator is. Do you:

1 Tell them to stop using bad language.
2 Tell them to ask the teacher.
3 Show them how to use an encyclopaedia.

Ulan Bator is the capital of Outer Mongolia, which shows education is much more relevant than in the days of transubstantiation and containers! I also like the cosy assumption that parents will have an encyclopaedia about the house.

The problem is that many parents who love their children also hate school. They have unhappy memories of their schooldays. Adrian Lee who worked as a teacher in New Cross felt he was involved in a constant war with some parents. In Adrian's school, parents thought it normal to let their children bunk off. Homework was for those who sucked up to the system. Teachers sometimes came under physical threat if they tried to discipline children. The National Union of Teachers claim this is a serious problem.

Some parents collude with their children against the school.

If this is how you feel, you need to be honest with yourself about it because your attitudes, conscious and unconscious, may damage your child's education severely.

And if some parents are hostile, others are too keen. History is littered with parents who tried to turn their little darlings into a genius and turned them into casualties instead. Judy Garland made her stage debut at the age of 2 because her mother had failed to become an actress and was utterly determined to make her daughter a star. Even Mozart reacted against the pressure of his pushy father.

Fathers need to strike a delicate balance. The child whose dad will look over homework when it is finished, the dad who will discuss what life was like under Mrs Thatcher for the project on mining, the dad who will talk about the news on television is helping. The dad who wants to know why you didn't come first, you lazy sod, will not help. There is a balance. Encourage, support but don't push.

If you failed to become Sean Connery or Richard Branson, don't expect your kids to do it for you.

The good enough father does not make his child 'a project'.

The absent father syndrome

After the Second World War, psychologists looked at how children whose fathers had been away fighting did at school and on intelligence tests. Absentee fathers damaged children intellectually and emotionally. Two factors were especially negative:

1 if the father is absent when the child is very young;

2 social class – working-class children are more affected than middle-class children by the father's absence.

A 1962 study looked at the family life of elementary-school boys who had average intelligence but who were 1 or 2 years behind at school. These boys had very poor relationships with their fathers; the fathers were inadequate and failed to achieve their own ambitions. Insecure and poor role models, they transmitted failure to their sons.

Radin *et al* (2000) found that both the quantity and quality of time fathers spent with their 4-year-old boys correlated with intelligence test scores on the Stanford Binet and the Peabody Picture Vocabulary Test. The strongest link was with so-called paternal nurturance. Children whose dad asked for information, children whose dad reached out to talk did much better. Studies of black girls and boys in elementary school found much the same. The more both parents interacted with the children, the better the girls and boys did on a number of cognitive tests. The father's behaviour was much more important than the mothers in affecting the boys.

Sutton Smith, a leading researcher on play, looked at the relationship between father absence and aptitude test scores among sophomores – 2nd-year college students in America. An absent father for Sutton Smith was a father who had not been there for two consecutive years. Children of these fathers did less well on verbal tests, on language tests and on general aptitude. Again the boys were hurt most.

It isn't just language that suffers either. A study of 500 children by Lessing *et al*. (1970) suggested the most dramatic effect of paternal deprivation was on perceptual motor and manipulative spatial tasks. Carlsmith (1964) found boys whose fathers had been absent for long periods answered questions in psychological tests more like girls did. With no male role model, these boys identified more with their mothers.

In Boston in America, black clergymen who work with the probation service argue that 95% of juvenile crime has 'fatherlessness' as a cause. The clergymen believe in a tough-love policy and claim they have helped reduce crime in the city; murders a year have fallen from 150 to 37. The reason for their success is telling; they believe the delinquents are desperate for fathering and so respond to a strong father figures.

Fathers matter, proved. But British families also face a curious cultural problem in dealing with education We have inhibitions about appearing to be intelligent or, even worse, intellectual.

Brains aren't for gentlemen

The Hungarian humorist, Georges Mikes, in his *How to Be an Alien* noted Britain is the only country where you can be criticised for being too intelligent. Mikes could never remember a Frenchman, a German or a Hungarian being sniped at for being 'too clever by half.' Yet, that's a perfect British barb. Bloggs is not sound, he's too clever by half. Swots were distrusted in public schools. The admired adolescent shone at cricket and passed exams without trying too hard. At Oxford till the 1970s, it was respectable to get a gentlemen's degree, a fourth. A third was sad, but a fourth showed you had not even bothered to try. Gentlemen just were – without trying.

Attitudes are changing but very slowly. Does this distrust of intellect have no connection with the fact Britain still has the worst literacy record in Europe? A record worse than Turkey? In most European countries, a minister of education who struggled to answer a simple mathematical question – what is 9×12? – would probably have been forced to resign. When David Blunkett took 13 seconds – longer than it takes an average sprinter to run

100 metres – to answer, no one suggested education might not be safe in his hands.

Parents & Schools reveals some curious attitudes. Quite sensibly, it gives nervous parents a list of 14 questions to ask teachers. These include 'Is there anything my child is particularly good at?' and 'What are they finding hard? How can I help'. Relentlessly cheery *Parents & Schools* never suggests, however, parents ask where their children are failing – and what they can do change that.

The shape of the individual mind

I believe parents have a better chance of helping their children intelligently if they understand the particular shape of their children's minds – and remember that a sibling may have a mind with a totally different shape.

I'll be personal again. My father had a real gift for languages. He spoke French, English, Hebrew, Arabic, some German and some Turkish. To the end of his days, he could quote long extracts from the Bible and the Koran.

On the other hand, if you asked my father to fix a plug, no hope! I am sure he never handled a screwdriver in his life. He never learned to drive. One of the more comic incidents in his life was when he ran a sandwich bar in Oxford Street. He was magnificent on how the Earl of Sandwich had created the sandwich; he could quote the lines about cucumber sandwiches from Oscar Wilde's *The Importance of Being Earnest*. But make a sandwich? Please . . .

I make a fine egg mayo even if I am a bit of an egghead. And I have inherited some of my father's lack of practical skills. While writing a book on psychological tests, I gave myself the Columbia Driving Skills Test, the best established paper and pencil test of driving aptitude. The cartoon gives you a good sense of the questions. I passed with flying colours.

Only I failed my driving test at the age of 17 on every count except parroting *The Highway Code*. While doing lessons before my second test, I had a life changing experience. Guildford Town Hall crashed into my vehicle. The Town Hall was driving far too fast straight at my mini. I gave up any driving ambitions.

Many people have gaps in their competence. Some 60 years ago in *The Normal Child*, C. W. Valentine confessed he could not remember names well. Shame for a clever man at the time, he also couldn't read Greek letters. Valentine also reported testing children who had an IQ of about 150 (i.e. in the top 1% of the population) but who could not recognise a tune. On the other hand, he had seen a perfectly average child who, at the age of 2, could sing back 63 different tunes.

In the 1980s, psychologists like Robert Ornstein, Robert Sternberg and Howard Gardner argued that, while a factor of general intelligence underlines all mental abilities, there are also more specialised intelligences. Ornstein called them 'modules' in the mind.

The author's driving experiences

For fathers, this kind of analysis is interesting. It means if you really want to understand your child, you need to get to know his or her strengths and weaknesses, all the modules of their mind.

Verbal, numerical, spatial, practical, musical, social, emotional intelligences all

The labels usually make it clear what skills are being tested.

Verbal intelligence

Those who score high will find crosswords, anagrams and other verbal plays fun and simple. They will like rhyming games. They can rejig the letters that comprise the word PATERNAL to make PARENTAL. They will know, almost automatically, that these words rhyme with RENTAL, DENTAL and MENTAL and, though the words are spelled differently, with GENTLE.

We live in a very verbal culture. Exams depend not just on what you know but how you can express it. Not surprisingly, verbal intelligence correlates highly with school and exam performance.

Numerical intelligence

Children with high scores on numerical IQ tend to do well in maths and sciences. But very large numbers of people have poor numerical skills. The Basic Skills Agency found in 1996 that only 20% of Britons could solve 12 simple mathematical questions like $5 - 1.78 =$ or $14 \times 11 =$ correctly.

Visuospatial intelligence

This is the ability to understand spatial relationships so that you can see that if you rotate figure X through 180 degrees you will get figure Y rather than Figure Z. This is the 'pure' intelligence component. In a culture like Britain's where design skills are in demand, such skills are becoming ever more important. If your child has good visuospatial skills and some numerical skills, it's a perfect if they want to be a web designer.

Musical intelligence

Obvious.

Practical intelligence

Though general intelligence affects it, we all know people who can pass exams and master the theory but are hopelessly impractical. Ask them to assemble an item of do-it-yourself furniture. I have seen intelligent men (i.e. me) driven to distraction by trying to assemble a DIY desk. I plan to write a paper on 'Sadism, Masochism and Self-Assembly Furniture'. Those who design it are sadists;

those who buy it knowing they will be unable to construct it are masochists.

Social intelligence

This is the ability to deal with other people and to understand their motives. There are some connections between this and the now fashionable 'emotional intelligence'.

Gardner, in particular, has stressed that some children with poor verbal and social skills show enormous talent in painting and drawing.

I am not suggesting you give your child an IQ test, but I do suggest you watch him or her. You will soon notice if they talk well, if they sing well, if they have a sense of how Lego fits together. Be open to their intellectual individuality. Be ready to spend time doing things they are really interested in.

But also be ready to be surprised. My neighbours were astonished when their shy 8-year-old daughter announced she was going to audition for a part in a London-wide musical project. Now they're delighted, proud and can't wait for the production. Performance abilities were the last thing they expected her to show.

If you see a problem (i.e. if your child has a poor vocabulary or is really clumsy), you can spend time on activities that are remedial but don't seem remedial. Who said parents never cheat? Again, it's a question of not being too direct, not teaching, but of spending time doing things that seem to be fun, are fun and will help deal with a particular problem.

All this requires finesse. Most 4- and 5-year-olds are sensitive and can often see what parents are trying to do and can resent it. Older children can be more defensive, so you have to be creative and not let this develop into a battle of wills. But be prepared to spend time on things your child finds hard and do it routinely, regularly and not in response to a crisis.

Vitamins and intelligence

Diet affects the brain. Children who are malnourished in the early years of life have lower IQ scores than average, though it's hard to be sure malnutrition is the only cause. Very deprived children are usually very deprived in a number of ways. Benton and Roberts (1988) triggered enormous interest with a small study. They gave a group of 30 Welsh children a vitamin and mineral supplement every day; at the end of 8 months, the experimental group had gained 10 points on a non-verbal IQ test while a control group who just got more attention only gained 2–4 points. Hans Eysenck told me that he was astonished when he reviewed the evidence by the positive impact of vitamins, especially vitamin C (Cohen, 1995). N. J. Mackintosh (1999) is more guarded saying 'legitimate doubts will not be dispelled until specific predictions (who will benefit, on what test, from what sort of supplementation) have been formulated and tested properly.'

Children need good food, not junk food. Small amounts of extra vitamins and minerals may not be a magic potion but, used sensibly, they won't do any harm.

Keeping tabs on school

Education is partly about routines. One good routine for fathers is to ask what happened at school from the first day a child attends. Sometimes, children won't want to talk. But if it is what you do when they start, it will become just part of the end of every day.

Always ask your child what they are doing at school. Sometimes, they will brush you off.

If he, or she, asks you to look at homework, do it and talk about what they got right, and what they got wrong.

If he, or she, asks you to do the homework, explain why there is no point in homework if you do it for them. Add that you are happy to look at the homework when it is done, and then to talk about it.

Always go to parent–teachers evenings. Remember parent–teacher evenings are held for the convenience of the school. If there isn't enough time to discuss something that is worrying you, insist on making an appointment so you can go back.

While it's important to encourage and support your child, be realistic. Do not expect your child to come top in everything or blame the school if she or he does not.

Attention-deficit disorder

Many parents feel their children can't concentrate. Often that's true. Small children, especially, do go from one thing to the next. It is part of their charm. But once a child goes to school, she or he has to be able to spend increasingly long periods of time at one task. It has been estimated that 15% of children have problems with concentration. Some are very impulsive, some are hyperactive, others just have 'attention deficits'. Usually these children – more often boys than girls – do badly at school.

In America, such children started to be diagnosed as psychiatric cases in the 1980s and there have been some signs of the trend spreading here. American doctors prescribed drugs like Ritalin in huge quantities to children as young as 6. Parents will find it very difficult to deal with a hyperactive child, but be careful before you agree to let your child go on medication of any kind for this. At the end of the book, I list organisations which offer advice on attention-deficit disorder and many suggest parents should first try various retraining methods which condition children, à la Skinner, to pay more attention.

Loads of logic

Piaget argued that, as they reach their teens, children become capable of sophisticated logical analysis. Piaget's 13-year-old, roughly the age when children start to master formal logical operations, is a terror but not for the usual reasons. (By formal operations, Piaget meant formal logical operations which concern propositions of the sort if p then q.) Piaget seemed to foresee the following kind of scenario.

You are just settling in to watch Arsenal v. Manchester Utd. You're ready for a real treat – chips, guacamole dip to be washed down with Guinness when Teenage Trouble struts in:

> **Trouble:** *I don't know how you can watch that rubbish, Dad.*

Dad: *Be nice to your dad ... shut up.*

Trouble: *You don't want to face the truth, Dad.*

This is a classic line. The teenager now accuses their parents of hypocrisy and selling out to the system. But Piaget's logical teenager isn't interested in existentials:

Trouble: *You are not drawing the logical conclusion, Dad.*

Dad: *Nor is the bloody Arsenal manager ...*

Trouble: *You always complain you're skint. Take the mortgage. You should have calculated that if there was a redemption penalty of 3% and a £2,000 cashback it was illogical for you to go for that product. The Save Your Pile Building Society has a lower cashback, a fractionally higher interest rate but a much smaller redemption penalty. Why can you never work things out logically? You're a pharmaceutical rep aren't you?*

Dad: *I certainly need drugs to cope with you ...*

Trouble: *Drug reps move on average every 3.8 years. You should have worked out you were likely to move during the period when the redemption penalty would hit.*

Dad: *I'm going to hit you. Who pays the bills in this house?*

Trouble: *I will soon. I've just signed a contract with*

*a leading City firm that recruits teenage
logicians. Loadsofmoney, loadsoflogic!*

Fortunately, research has shown that virtually no one
becomes Piaget's logical paragon. One study found it
was 1 in 76 teenagers. Exceptions are those who become
professional mathematicians. If your child cross-exam-
ines you as above, I have little to suggest other than
going to live in South America as soon as possible.

Talk is good

Talk with your children. Talk like the man on the No. 15
bus did with his son. Talk football, hard rock, design, *Big
Brother*, Tony Blair, Shrek, Madonna, whatever, as long
as you share your ideas and experiences. You can even talk
about television programmes.

One other benefit of having a sense of the shape of
your child's mind is that you can avoid ...

The father–child mismatch disaster

If you are an intensely practical person who likes to go
fishing and fix motorcycles and you have 10-year-old
style-wise daughter who wants to be a dress designer
and can tell a McQueen from a Dior, you have a real
problem. Do you go shopping with her which will be
hell for you? Do you try to teach her how to fix motor
bikes which she'll probably refuse to do? Or do you com-

promise creatively? She has a high visual IQ, is interested in design and so talk to her about doing something – neither bikes nor frocks – that you can both get fun out of doing together. Creative compromise with our kids is not always that easy but it's worth trying.

Sometimes, a father's lot is not a happy one. He does not get the credit. Both my children can cook. I believe this was due to my example. Since they were tiny, they have seen me in the kitchen, displaying practical intelligence, slaving at the ratatouille, soupe à l'onion, delice de saumon, steak au poivre, not to mention the 'Stir Fry de Mincemeat avec Legumes which Happen to be in Fridge and not Mouldy'. My rotten sons claim that, given how I cook, it's a miracle they are still alive and they can put spaghetti bolognese together.

Finally, I want to return to time. Many fathers feel work is so demanding that they cannot give their children the time they need.

Time

Even the most workaholic executive is not gone for 2 years like men were during the war. But many men do feel guilty about being away, as a number of Dutch fathers confessed in *Unravelling Fatherhood*. One said:

> *I am dissatisfied about being so little at my children's disposal, mainly because of my job. It takes so much of my energy away than I am not in the mood to occupy myself intensively with the children. I am dissatisfied.*

The National Childbirth Trust survey found 40% of men said they had to work too hard to really play their part as a father. A labourer said 'Because of the lack of sleep it affects my work and I can't concentrate. If I make mistakes I could lose my job but my wife still wants me to get up at night for feeds.' A salesman told the survey 'I worry about finding a balance between work and our newborn. Everything has slowed down to at least half speed.'

Only 50% of the fathers in the survey had had any paternity leave and it was usually between 2 and 5 days. Jack O'Sullivan of Fathers Direct argues many fathers are upset about having to go back to work so soon after the birth. The average British male works 45 hours. In London and the South-East, you probably have to add at least 1 hour to 90 minutes in travel time. Total time away from home between 55 and 60 hours – 2.5 days in a 5 day week.

Time is a problem, but the week is 168 hours long. This still leaves fathers with a staggering 108 hours to sleep, go to the pub and do things with their children. And that is before we make any attempt to reschedule time.

Balance is everything. Do not get too stressed by your child's successes or failures at school. I am very struck by the opinion of a friend of mine who has had a rather distinguished career – and four children. 'As long as the children are happy,' says David Hunt who was in the Cabinet. Unfortunately perhaps, David was never, however, Secretary of State for Education.

You're not my real dad – stepfathers and part-time fathers

Angel is 16 years old. She's got a dumpy, doughy face. She puffs away at her roll-your-own. She's an Essex girl; she's obviously told her life before to counsellors and other experts. It's a sad tale. Her father died when she was 10. Her mother was depressed for a long time, but then she took up with a man Angel liked. He bought her Bounty bars and Angel liked sitting on his knee 'like a real daughter'. He never came on to her. Angel just loved the affection. She hadn't had much of it.

But her good stepfather wasn't around for long. Her mother threw him out because she was fed up with his drinking. Angel was sad, her mother 'then took up with a new bloke.' He was a bit younger and there were endless rows between him and Angel. 'I thought he was a tosser,' she told me. But her mother liked him. The rows got too much and, just before she was 15, Angel ran away from home.

When she went back after a few days, 'mum made me feel it'd been better when I wasn't there.' Angel felt depressed and then she started hearing voices. Voices that

frightened her. Her mother said she couldn't stand all the
rowing between Angel and her new man. Angel just left
again. She spends her time between hostels and the
streets. She's got a drug habit. She likes that. She was
calm when we met in a hostel, still angry about her
mother but calm. She has no idea if her mother misses
her. Her mum is still with her younger bloke and Angel
won't set foot in the house while he's around. Angel is one
of thousands of casualties of stepfamily life.

Some research suggests that 50% of stepchildren hate
their stepfathers. It's a worrying statistic when one British
marriage in two ends in divorce. The figures issued by
Stepfamily, the national organisation, seem almost low;
they estimate there are between 2.5 and 3 million stepfamilies in the UK. The stepmother and stepfather are no
longer exotic fairy-tale characters.

Given these numbers, we have to be surprised by how
little research has been done on stepfamilies, how they
function and what can be done to make those who live
in them happier. In this chapter, I deal with some of the
obvious problems stepfathers face and compare these with
those of part-time fathers. I try also to give some basic
advice on how to smooth the process of 'blending' families
together. The jargon talks now of 'blended' or 'reconstituted' families – foodie metaphors gone mad. But families
are complicated, individual and defy general rules.

Too little research into stepfamilies

Gill Gorell Barnes and her colleagues at the Tavistock
Institute have recently published a study of 444 children
born in 1958, some 50 of whom were brought up in step-

families (Gorell Barnes, 1998). They studied how the stepfamily worked and especially the long-term impact on children. Gorell Barnes points out that the main previous study was of a group of stepfamilies in Sheffield (Burgoyne, 1984). American and Australian researchers have looked at larger samples over longer periods of time but, given the millions of children who grow up as, 'steps', we know far too little about the subject.

The children Gorell Barnes studied became stepchildren in the 1960s when divorce still carried considerable stigma. The divorce law changed in Britain in 1967. Before then, one party had to prove the other guilty of adultery, desertion or mental cruelty. If your parents were divorced, you often did not tell your friends at school. Today, in theory, stepfamilies don't face that kind of shame, they're just one more part of our multicultural multi-sexual social weave. We don't know if; or how, that culture change has affected either stepchildren or step-parents.

There's nothing new in what my ex-wife nicely calls 'baroque' family situations, however. The Bible is full of them including Abraham having at least two wives and, with the help of the Lord, getting Sarah pregnant long after she should have been barren. In the less biblical 18th century, Dr Johnson observed second marriages are a triumph of hope over experience. Gorell Barnes points out that many famous men like Isaac Newton were stepchildren. Newton may have discovered the laws of physics, but he had a miserable personal life, some very odd ideas and poor personal hygiene.

We get a good sense of how family dynamics may not have changed by looking at the story of the French poet, Charles Baudelaire. In 1831, 10-year-old Charles Baudelaire was introduced by his mother to his new 'father', General Aupick. Baudelaire's real father had died; his mother had fallen in love, but she had not told

her son that his life was about to change. Biographers
disagree about General Aupick. Some see him as honour-
able but misguided; others give him the familiar role of
the step-monster. The General did take his stepson on a
trip to the Pyrenees which led to Baudelaire's first published poem, *Incompatibility*. But then the General
seemed to want to put as much distance as possible
between Charles and the family. He arranged for his
stepson to take a character-building trip to India. For
much of the voyage, however, Charles locked himself in
his cabin in protest. He then accused the General of poi-
soning his relationship with his mother. Then, there was
the issue of money. The General had denied him his substantial inheritance of 75,000 francs, Charles claimed, and
had been much nicer to his creepy, goody-goody half-
brother.

In other words, it's naive to think stepfamily stress is
postmodern stuff. But General Aupick had some Victorian blessings. He doesn't seem to have had to cope with his
first wife being constantly on the phone to complain the
cheque for the alimony didn't seem to have arrived just
yet.

Stress and stepdads

Today's stepfather has to live with stress and irony. He
may be living with a new partner and her children, but
only seeing his biological children on a part-time basis.
His children live with their mother most of the time. And
she has a new bloke. Under the same roof, we can find the
following:

- biological father/biological child;
- stepfather/stepchild;
- biological mother/biological child;
- stepmother/stepchild;
- brother/sister;
- stepbrother/stepsister.

It takes deep social and emotional skills to deal with such a mix of relationships, especially when many of those involved will have been hurt. The children will feel hurt because they have been abandoned by their true father. Whether he died, left or was finally kicked out, children will usually mourn and miss the old man. Gorell Barnes found mothers were better than fathers at preparing children for a new relationship, but even they were often secretive and embarrassed. Children do not like seeing their parents as sexual beings. So nobody tells them about the new man or the new woman till they absolutely have to.

Children often were confused, Gorell Barnes found. When a parent left, sometimes, they did not know what had happened to their real mothers or fathers, or when, or if, they would ever see them again. Gorell Barnes reports one child as typical. She said her mum just introduced 'us to this new man one day and said he was going to be living with us.' Ace emotional intelligence there.

In the 1960s, Britain was still very deferential. Children knew their place. Few ever dreamed of complaining; parents were totally right; no one talked about abuse or neglect or children's rights. Expectations of stepfathers were also low, Gorell Barnes found. They were men after all, and men didn't do much round kids. A stepfather was not usually called dad. Many children saw the stepdad 'more as an uncle'; he got involved but not that involved. He would sometimes help by looking over homework and take them out for a spin in the car as a treat. But he wasn't like a real dad. He was much more detached and had much less of a voice in discipline. It's a bit hard to know how to take these findings because so much research suggests that, till the 1980s, biological dads weren't very different. It is a pity that we can't compare Gorell Barnes' thorough data with research on contemporary stepfamilies.

It is not just children in a new stepfamily who feel hurt, however. New relationships are constructed on old baggage. A new couple builds on two ex-couples and all their sorrows, angers, frustrations. In any stepfamily house, as well as the physical presences there are the in-visibles – her ex, his ex. Often, when there are battles about access and custody, these ex's are very present. And they can wound – through the mouths of babes even when the babes don't mean it. A stepchild says, 'don't you know I hate peanut butter' when you unpack the shopping. Pain. You remember your real son loves peanut butter but your ex and her new macho man have got him 88% of the time. The last time he came here for the weekend, he hated her children and ended up going for a walk by himself. Your precious weekend with him became a nightmare.

Gorell Barnes found many stepchildren said they hated the new stepfather, but they had to recognise their mother was less tense and happier than before. Children as young as 8 realised that the situation they found painful was also giving their mother, whom they loved, real joy.

In a stepfamily, everyone has to cope with new people who have new habits. In theory we should be able to treat this as an adventure. If we learn to work together, we'll all be happy. But human beings find it hard to make such win–win situations come true for them.

Trust versus mistrust

The psychoanalyst Erik Erikson looked at the choices children make, and have made for them, at crucial points in development. The first 'choice' is trust versus mistrust. If a baby cries and is picked up and comforted, he or she will learn from that and hundreds of other experiences to trust. If the baby is left to cry when she's hungry or dirty, she will tend towards distrust. A stepchild has, in all likelihood, already lived through hard times which will promote distrust. He, or she, also doesn't know you, and will probably have met you in tense circumstances. Everything you can do to create trust is likely to help. But don't expect a grateful little toddler. You are dealing with a child who is probably angry and likely to rebuff you.

Authors of children's books are well aware of that dynamic. With millions of stepfamilies, a niche market has developed in books about how families 'blend'. In them, the steps are not the evil weirdos of fairy tales. The hilariously titled *Living with My Stepfather is Like Living with a Moose* and *The Stepman*, have similar plots. At first, the children hate the stepfather but, slowly, they come to see he's a nice man who has his odd habits but who loves their mother. He's not a monster. They will let him hug them, he's all right. Happiness all round.

In real life, winning trust is not easy. It is hard especially when children are hurt or confused. Stepfathers themselves have often been through experiences which make them mistrust. In one way, laying down rules is arrogant but there are two simple ones I believe are nearly always right.

Do not slag off their real father even if their mother complains about him. You wouldn't want to be slagged off in front of your own children. The exception is if their real father is being abusive or violent.

Be consistent in the amount of emotion and warmth you offer. It's no good one weekend being committed and the next acting as if well you're not really my children.

Above all, spend time with your new children and talk to them because how else can you get to know them and they get to know you. As we get to know the children and they get to know us, love will start.

But if that starts to happen, it brings a subtle problem. How much of a father do you become to them? This can be specially difficult when the children are really small. Often, men have to find a difficult balance between not pretending to be the real dad and, yet, at the same time, being a good enough most of the time parent.

Historically, step-parents have not done well. Step-children do less well at school and they tend to be less well adjusted. Gorrell Barnes found that many of her sample left home early and married early. They were looking for emotional stability, but far more than average they tended to get divorce. So a cycle of unhappiness set in.

The rules of the house

Alex was 16 and Katy was 18 when their mother Julia and I set up house together in Camden Town. Douglas Ross, their father, had died tragically young in the Highlands 12 years earlier. Julia got a new job in London and decided to take it. Katy and Alex had very different reactions to the move. Katy loved London and did not really mind leaving Scotland; Alex minded badly. He was a Scot and was very aware of his father's love for his country. Katy spoke

Home Counties even though she had lived in Edinburgh all her life. Alex had a Scottish accent. He found London hard, especially as he had to cope, he said, with a lot of anti-Scots feeling.

Alex insisted he went to boarding school. His mother, who was desperate to make him feel happy, agreed. I found it hard to talk to him in the way that I did to my sons. I didn't know him well enough to ask what might have been useful questions. Just why did he want to go to boarding school? Was he trying to avoid living with us? We weren't interested in the same things and I didn't try as hard as I should have done.

So, Alex went off for a year to Kings Canterbury. My two sons lived part-time with us, commuting between our house and their mother's. As all the children were young adults, we did not have some battles that are familiar in stepfamilies with younger children.

With small children, 'new families' battles are often practical as well as psychological. You and your new partner may have different styles of discipline. You may be a traditional father who believes his word is law. But your new partner's children are used to a more relaxed father who let them stay up much later. If you don't insist her children go to bed at 9 p.m, what will happen when your kids come to stay? You can't tell them to go to bed if the others are staying up.

Box 9   Typical flashpoints

What happens if dinner includes something one of the children hates like fish pie? Do you cook something different for the awkward squad?

Who gets to choose the TV we watch?

What are the rules about doing homework?

What are the rules about bedtime? In one family, 6-year-olds go to bed at 9 p.m and are never allowed to stay up later. In another, they go to bed at 8.30 but if there is something special on TV they can stay up later.

What are the rules about going into the parents' bedroom?

The list is not exhaustive but when you are trying to bring two families together, adults and children both need clarity. The trouble is that is it is even harder than usual to get emotional clarity when a new stepfamily is starting because it is an emotional time. One possible solution is to have House Council and Curry.

You are treating or bribing the children blatantly, but you are doing so for a good reason: they need to listen and speak. Order an Indian takeaway. If that's too expensive, agree with your partner to cook something special. Get everyone relaxed and then explain the rules of the House Council and Curry – don't call it a family council because that allows her children to say 'where's my real daddy' and your children to say 'where's my real mummy?'

Talking is the only solution. You are all in this together. You need to sit down and work out what the new rules of the new house are. Then tell the children what you think are fair rules for the kinds of situations described above. Then give them the chance to protest, to change your mind, to listen, to raise other issues. Adapted for stepfamily life, these are very much the principles which Watson recommended and on which A. S. Neill ran his school at Summerhill. If they suggest something silly, laugh. Nothing should be taboo in the House Council. Then write up the Rules of the House on a noticeboard and put it somewhere where all can read.

This won't magic-cure all problems, but it does set out rules and creates an atmosphere in which children know talk and negotiation is possible. Promise yourselves to hold such a Council once a month because there will be blow-ups in stepfamily life.

The adults had better work out a consistent position on, at the very least, the following:

- What is punished?
- How is it punished?
- What kind of behaviour gets encouraged or praised or rewarded?

Children do have a sense of fairness, according both to Piaget's work and that of Kohlberg. And most children hate being left in the dark. If your Harriet is smacked when she is rude to her new stepmum while her Tina gets away with just a telling off when she is rude to you, the children will feel worse than confused. You will have raised some of the most painful spoken and unspoken questions in the stepfamily situation.

- Do you love me as much?
- Do you love him or her more?
- Why do you love me less?

These questions are at the root of most anguish. Avoid
them by being loving and fair.

A room at the top

Julia's mother, Anita, came with us to look at the house in
Camden after we had made an offer for it. Anita found it
hard to climb stairs because she had a heart condition, but
she had noticed on the estate agent's particulars that there
was a huge room on the top floor. Julia wanted Alex to
have this room, partly because she felt guilty about bringing him down from Scotland. Julia's mother, who loved
Alex dearly, 'ummed' in a significant way. What would
the other children feel, she asked, if Alex had this splendid
room. Apart from the master bedroom, it was the best
bedroom in the house.

Anita suggested we divide the room into two. But Alex
was the youngest, the one who had hated the move most.
So he got the best room to make him feel better. It didn't
lead to any big battles but it could have easily done so if all
the children had been living at home all the time. Jealousy
is always lurking in families and, even more in stepfamilies.

Making your children and stepchildren feel they are
all loved, loved equally, and loved for the fact that they are
all different is not easy. You will almost certainly not love
your stepchildren as much as your children. You've
known your own children longer for a start, but you can
make stepchildren feel secure – and make sure their
mother shows them how much she loves them. Parents
often admit that they have a favourite child. I've always
been surprised, even shocked by this. But I think it is even
more important in a stepfamily to give all the children a

sense they are equal and treated the same. Injustices don't help love grow.

Co-parenting problems

Studies suggest there are three different kinds of parenting after divorce and/or separation:

- **positive and co-operative co-parenting** where mother and father can still communicate well about the children;
- **absent parenting** when one person is not there and so the all the responsibility falls on one person;
- **hostile co-parenting**. Prof. Jackie Walker of Newcastle University, who led a major research programme on divorce and mediation for the Lord Chancellors Department, recently warned lawyers and social workers not to be too optimistic. In a quarter of cases where parents appear to co-operative for the sake of the children the best you can get is hostile acquiescence.

Faced with such situations, it's not surprising that some stepfathers hit on strange survival strategies. One of the my favourites is Brian who has a website.

How to survive as a stepdad

Brian of Stepfamilies Are Us says that, while he still loves his biological children, his first loyalty is now to his new woman. Brian has now become mature enough to be selfish. He owes it to himself. Brian only gets to see his biological child on weekends while his new mate and her child are there every day of the week. So, that's very understandable then.

I believe putting yourself in a position where you have to choose between your partner and your children is a counsel of despair. Despite the conflicts, you can be a good father, a good stepfather and a good new husband or new partner. In my 5 years in a stepfamily, I've learned you need love, patience, negotiating skills, the occasional 'I am finally now going to put my foot down' and the also occasional ride to the rescue. You can't manage this if you're not prepared to be honest with yourself – and look at your behaviour. And that again means asking tough questions.

Box 10   Do you favour your own children?

In what kind of situations do you favour your children?

What annoys you about your stepchildren?

Are you likely to lose your temper more easily with your stepchildren than with your own children?

If so, what can you do about it?

What do you like about your stepchildren?

> Would you rather live in a situation where they were not always there – getting between you and your new partner? Some of Gorell Barnes's subjects said they hated seeing physical affection between their mother and the new stepfather.
>
> Is there any hobby or activity you can share with one or more of your stepchildren?

I am not suggesting you change into a saint and I certainly don't claim I did, but you need to analyse your behaviour scrupulously and see what you can do to change it. If your relationship with your new partner is good, you should be able to talk to her about these problems, especially as she is likely to have similar difficulties in coping with your own children.

Why socks don't obey the laws of gravity but their movements can also be explained

There are no easy fixes and if you are an uptight person you may find yourself in difficult situations. As you read on, remember to be glad you are not related to Isaac Newton who may have solved the mysteries of gravity but hated soap apparently.

Katy and Alex were both in their late teens when I started to live with their mother. My sons sometimes stayed with us and, sometimes, with their mother. My sons have never believed that socks or, in Nicholas's case, underpants are private property. There is a store of socks and knickers in London and you help yourself wherever necessary. So my sons nick socks belonging to my new partner's children. They take them back to their mother's house who doesn't quite understand why she's washing Alex Ross's socks. My sons also nick their mother's partner's socks and, it was eventually revealed, his underwear. I am sympathetic to the socks-belong-to-everyone philosophy, so I have found myself wearing socks that belong to my ex-wife's new man. But never his pants. We still have some standards. Experts on blended or reconstituted families have not yet focused on the sock phenomenon.

The part-time dad

I've said nothing so far about a situation many men find themselves in – being a part-time father. Groups like Families Need Father stress the need for part-time fathers to be treated fairly by the law when it comes to access, child support and the education of the children. This is not a legal book and men who are divorcing or separating need good legal advice. At the end of the book, I list organisations which are helpful.

But when it comes to how you behave towards your child or children, there is very little difference between being a good enough part-time father and a good enough full-time father. But the part-time father feels under great pressure. He may be isolated. He may feel great bitterness; the divorce, the ex-wife, her new man have ruined his life and, on top of it, robbed him of his children.

I once filmed at an access centre, a centre specially designed for fathers who could not be trusted alone with their children. Usually, that was because either social services or the courts felt there was a risk of violence, abuse or of abduction. Two Saturday mornings a month, Sam was allowed to see his 3-year-old son there. The centre was in a bleak building in Croydon. It was fitted out with a few toys and a rather jolly tube that children could crawl through. Sam's ex was in no mood to listen when she brought their child to him. She had had enough of being scared by him. She was glad she didn't have to be frightened. Sam was bitter. But once she had gone, Sam managed to put his anger to one side and romped in and out of the tube with his son for hours. At the end, when he had to hug his son goodbye, the bad feelings came back. But his son hadn't noticed.

Lawyers will advise on how to increase access and you should try to negotiate increased access. Often mothers will be receptive if only because it gives them time by themselves – and most parents also want that. Somehow, you need to find the strength to ... See the end of the book for details of organisations that can help.

Freud and violence

I'm afraid, yet again we have to consider the Oedipus complex and violence.

Try to think as the Oedipal child thinks, consciously and unconsciously. Are you, the stepfather, the man who is now spending the night in his mother's bed? Where his father used to be? Where the boy fantasises unconsciously about being? You don't kill your father because he is bigger and you have started to identify with him, but since your father probably wants your stepfather killed ... I'm talking unconscious here ... the child has every unconscious right to be angry, even violent. And, yet, there are few cases of stepfathers being murdered.

The statistics show the reverse. Usually, it is step-fathers who are violent – not stepchildren. And the statistics are worrying. Physical child abuse by step-fathers is frequent according to the NSPCC. They point out that each week 600 new children are added to the official child-protection register in England and Wales. 26% of all rapes are committed against children. Some Canadian research is frightening because it shows how, even in extreme situations, men behave very differently towards their biological children and their stepchildren.

Margo Wilson and Martin Daly of McMaster University have studied 239 cases of family wipe-out where men kill their wives and children. Wilson and Daly found the background nearly always reveals men kill their wives or girlfriends because the women are a little too independent. 'If I can't have her, then nobody can,' is how they characterise the thinking. George Palermo, another expert in this macabre field and the editor of the *International Journal of Offender Therapy*, speaks of paranoid jealousy. And that jealousy often seals the fate of the children too. Wilson and Daly were struck by the fact that, in other species, fathers rarely kill their offspring. Hyenas are, apparently, an exception.

In humans, murder is the last resort, by which the threatened man exerts control. In many of the 239 Canadian deaths, the woman was either having a relationship with another man, threatening to leave the marriage or had already walked out.

In family wipe-outs, stepchildren are four times more likely to suffer violence from stepfathers than biological children. Men do protect their genes.

It's very important for men who feel they cannot cope with stepfamily tensions to get help.

I know I've painted a rather bleak picture, with much stress, but many stepfamilies do succeed. We need far more research into how to make stepfamilies work better because every prediction about society in the future suggests there will be more and more of them.

Heartache

In 2001, James Lawson got a suspended sentence for manslaughter. His daughter was desperately depressed. She begged him to help her to die because she could no longer take it. The Lawson family had seen her struggle with depression for years. Finally, James Lawson suffocated his daughter. He was given a suspended sentence on the grounds of diminished responsibility. Passing sentence, the judge said he could not imagine a more tragic crime.

In Jewish folklore, you never praise a child too much in case the angels decide to snatch such a paragon away.

I have been lucky so far. Our two worst accidents were serious but not life threatening – a broken arm and a bitten nose. When Nicholas was 9 months old, he and his grandmother's dog were fighting for a piece of cake under the kitchen table. The dog had bitten before, but all the children in the family were scared he would be put down. So they never told their parents when it happened

Nicholas was rushed to hospital and had to have plastic surgery. He spent his first Xmas in a straitjacket to stop him scratching the skin graft off his nose. Once the immediate emergency was over, Aileen and I realised we were lucky. At worst, Nicholas would have a bad scar. The other children kept in hospital over Xmas were desperately sick or dying; the rest had gone home to be with their families.

In Britain, 220 children die each year in road accidents – and there was a 7% rise in 2000. Car crashes, drownings, road accidents, leukaemia, meningitis, the ways death can get your children are infinitely various. I cannot give a reasonable account of all the possible nightmares parents may have to face in a chapter. (There is a list of self-help groups at the end of book, however.)

Instead, I concentrate on mental health and stress because it has been argued they really are the greatest health threat for young people today. In 1997, the House of Commons Select Committee on mental-health (2001) heard that 40% of British children might have some form of mental-health problem. Recently, it has been suggested that every school should have a mental-health worker in residence. The *Journal of the American Academy of Child Psychiatry* lists a variety of mental-health problems children and young people suffer including hyperactivity, schizophrenia, psychosis, mania, eating disorders, suicide, attempted suicide, alcohol and drug abuse, depression; the journal also carries studies of juvenile serial killers. The latest UK government report in 2001 claims not 40% but that one in five young people 'has' some sort of mental-health problem.

That simple sentence masks a major shift in attitudes and not a good one. The sentence assumes that if a child is, for example, depressed, it is their condition just as it would be their condition if they had the mumps. But Britain was a pioneer of child guidance and family therapy from the 1920s at clinics like the Tavistock. The philosophy was simple. If a child had psychological problems, we should examine the whole family and its dynamics. A child's mental health can't be seen in isolation. This sensible approach is being ditched. There are obvious reasons for this shift, the tabloid tales of young men out of control, pessimism about therapy and rehabilitation, a punitive culture. But to harp on just the sick child denies the complexity of family dynamics. Stress does not happen in a vacuum. Even if a child is depressed because he is being bullied at school, we need to ask why his parents seem so powerless to help him.

Cracking younger

Peter Wilson, an ex-social worker who runs the mental-health charity Young Minds told me:

> *There's enough evidence to suggest that mental-health problems have been on the increase in the last 30 years or so. There's pretty good empirical evidence of that. If you talk to people who work with children ... in schools, in clinics, social workers who deal with some of the more distressing aspects of life ... most of them will say that the problems are more complicated, more extreme, more pressing and children seem to be more agitated, more fractious, more disorganised and are not sure where they are.*

Many consultant child psychiatrists agree.

No one is sure if, in the past, doctors ignored depressed children or whether the pressures on children have increased so much they crack younger. Dr Andrew

Clark, a consultant at the Prestwich Adolescent Unit which has 15 beds for teenagers told me:

> *Children from eight years upwards can give an account of a depressive episode. They feel horrible inside, they feel their friends think they're no good, they don't want to get up in the morning, life isn't worth living. Unless you talk to the young people you don't get these accounts. Parents and teachers are very good at telling what young people do and don't do but they're not good at telling you how it feels inside that young person.*

The state of young depression

Tony is the 11-year-old son of a designer. She's a single mother and is very amusing. She used to talk lovingly about her son – the pleasures and problems of being a single parent.

Between 1999 and 2000, she became desperately worried because her son had become depressed. That wasn't like him at all. She tried to get him to talk. He just clammed up. She got irritated. She took time off so that they would have time together. Still she couldn't get him to explain. He just repeated that nothing was wrong. But Tony often just refused to get up. Making him go to school was a daily battle. Once, he enjoyed sports, especially tennis and football. Now, he couldn't be bothered to play.

Tony's mother took him to the doctor who was baffled. Baffled doctors reach for drugs. She hated the idea of her son being medicated. But she didn't know what else to do. When he became depressed, he was a blank and that blankness frightened her. Tony became more and more withdrawn.

She gathered as much information as she could from the Internet and other sources about drugs. She found out that, in the States, so-called Baby Prozac is very popular. There was a point when Tony felt suicidal – and let his mother know it. She blamed herself and she felt frustrated. They had a good relationship so why couldn't she get him to talk to her? Tony was not stupid, he wasn't unable to express his feelings. She tried to give him treats to cheer him up. All her love, all her intelligence were defeated. She was in despair. His depression had made her depressed – and she knew that was dangerous.

Suicide and attempted suicide

The suicide statistics are also stark. The rate of suicide for young men under 18 has risen dramatically since the 1970s. In 1970, there were 7 cases of suicide per 100,000; in 1991. there were 16.4 per 100,000. Boys as young as six have made attempts. In addition, there were over 220 suspicious accidental deaths which might have been suicide. Often suicide notes blame bullying at school. Ten-year-old Dijendra, who was bullied at school, hanged himself. His family were surprised and blamed the school for failing to protect them. The inquest at Southwark returned an open verdict. Yet, they seemed to have little idea at home how depressed Dijendra was by being bullied.

In addition to 'successful' suicides, there are thousands of attempted suicides. One recent estimate is 150,000 a year. Are there important differences between young people who succeed in killing themselves, those

who 'just' make attempts and those who self-harm? Sally
O'Brien, who wrote a fine book called *The Negative
Scream*, warns against assuming that there are and that
those who cry for help will never really do it.

Sometimes, parents become exhausted by the psychological games and tension. Twenty years ago, I interviewed Rebecca who was then in her late teens. She had
made 13 suicide attempts. She spoke of feeling better after
she had cut herself. One attempt had its funny side. She
had gone topless into the sea at Clacton, yelling 'Jimmy
I'm coming to join you.' Jimmy was her husband who, as
Rebecca's mother acidly pointed out, had managed to kill
himself at his first attempt throwing himself with perfect
timing under a tube train. In Clacton, the will-Rebecca-
die-or-not saga drew police, the coastguard and an audi-
ence of agog tourists. Rebecca was dragged out of the sea.
She could tell the story with some irony at her own
expense. But her mother couldn't see the humour. She
was too tired, too sceptical. Rebecca had got what she
wanted, even more attention than usual.

But suicide attempts often do not have that black
humour edge. In 1998, I met Judy and Susan at a psychiatric unit for teenagers in Prestwich. She was a tall
articulate 18-year-old girl who, had only been admitted
after making a serious suicide attempt. Judy had improved by the time I filmed. She was taking part in art
therapy and I recorded a discussion she had with Kate
Kellett (the art therapist) and two other girls about why
they self-harmed:

Judy: *I just do it because I hate myself and I think
I deserve it.*

Kate: *You deserve to be punished in what way?*

Judy: *Yeah.*

Kate: *That's different from the way it's for you [looking at Susan].*

Kate now turned to a very depressed girl who was 16. Her wrists and lower arms were a mass of cuts and razor slashes. She had three bandages on:

Susan: *It's always the voices that start it off, they say.*

Earlier in the week Susan had asked the art therapist to get razors for her. Kate had refused. It was Judy, who had some insight, who made the point:

Judy: *She's supposed to help so how would you feel if she just said 'Go for it'?*

Kate: *It's hypothetical but think it through.*

Susan: *In the long run I know it's bad but in the short term, given the way that I feel now, I'd think Thank God here's someone who understands how what's going on.*

Judy: *I know it's a solution but it's not the solution to get you better.*

Kate: *You know that, don't you?*

Susan: *There's a bit of me that knows that it's not right but then the voices start saying to me and the bigger part of me say you know you've got*

to do it. It's an impossible situation. It's incred-
ibly hard to stop once you've done it. Even if I
didn't do for years I'd always have to come
back to it eventually.

Later in the session Susan made a lumpy clay figure with a
big smile. She described him:

Like a guardian ... There are so many bad guys ...
we could do with some good guys to help me to fight the
voices. It makes me feel good, helping to create
someone who could help me. I know he can't really
but it feels like it could help.

Susan's feelings – depression, despair, anger and a need
for release – are easy to reel off in the abstract. But thousands of teenagers are hit by them every day, every night
and often they can't pinpoint just what they are triggered
by. (Judy and Susan are not the real names.)

As frightening for parents to deal with are hallucinations.

Voices

Until recently, psychiatrists believed there were few cases
of schizophrenia before the age of 16. Late teens was the
classic age of onset. Now, child psychiatrists find evidence of children having psychotic breakdowns much
younger. Dr Clark and his colleagues at Prestwich said
they had seen children aged between 8 and 10 who

heard voices and had many of the symptoms of schizophrenia. Roughly 1% of the population develop schizophrenia – it is a major illness.

Heredity does give some people a predisposition to schizophrenia. A gene for schizophrenia has been found and there are brain abnormalities in many sufferers. But many people, whose heredity predisposes them to the disease, never develop it. Partly because they don't have to deal with the stresses that can trigger the onset of the disease attack. That stress can be caused by problems with fathers and stepfathers.

When Sarah was first sent to Brookside, a therapeutic community just outside Romford, she presented as a classic schizophrenic. She was 14 and already she was hearing voices. Scary voices that she refused to describe. The Brookside team had no idea what had led to this. There was no schizophrenia in the family. Sarah was usually rather withdrawn. The clinic took time to unravel a traumatic but confused background.

Sarah had seen her father die and blamed herself for his death. It was not clear whether her mother blamed her for her father's death. It seemed unlikely. Rather, inexplicably, Sarah turned a tragedy into something she was alone responsible for. She was 13 at the time – and the voices started then. Her mother mourned her loss, but eventually she did make a new relationship. It didn't work well. The man was violent. Sarah watched her mother being beaten up by the new bloke. Now Sarah blamed herself for her mother being beaten up. Sarah disliked the man but there was nothing to suggest he disliked her.

Paul Caviston, Brookside's consultant psychiatrist, told me that there were, of course, many children who saw their mothers being beaten and lived through other extreme and traumatic experiences. But many children who experience through similar traumas cope and do not start hearing voices. Just why some did develop psychotic symptoms remained something of a mystery.

On the other hand, some children are upsetting, partly because they are so good at expressing their anger.

Anger

Emma, a 13-year-old girl, was in the Prestwich Adolescent Unit for assessment. Since the age of 10, she had worried her school and her mother because she gets so angry. Emma had no idea why. She was fed up with all the 'talk' in the unit. The talk didn't help her. Staff often say the problem is that children can't express their feelings. Emma seems able to say what's bothering her perfectly well. She's bored and angry. She doesn't reckon she has much of a life when the most exciting thing she does is visit Tesco's, without money to spend. When her mother came to visit, they had a going-in-circles row. Emma wanted £2.79 to buy fags; her mother refused to give it to her. Emma started tearing her clothes up. Her mother told her not to do that.

Emma continued tearing her clothes up. Her mother said that was no way to get pocket money. She is a single mother, grossly overweight and on benefit, a woman with her own problems.

Emma calculated that her mother owed her pocket money and that, anyway, her mother was saving money. While Emma was in the Unit, Mum spent less on food. Emma said her mother loved her three sisters more; the mother said she was fed up with Emma and just wanted to know what was wrong with her.

Emma and her mother are engaged in an extreme teenage battle. Emma is 'lucky' in that she has not been put on medication. One reason, I suspect, is that while she is very provocative, she is also very articulate. And the person she is most provocative to is her mother not medical staff.

Is it right to label?

The famous antipsychiatrist R. D. Laing (1927–1989) argued society is all too ready to label any odd behaviour as mad. Laing never dealt with children, however. Some doctors like Adrian Sutton, a psychoanalyst and a psychiatrist in Manchester, echo his views. Sutton thinks it is wrong to hang labels like 'psychotic' on children as young as eight. But he also told me he has seen children of that age with 'psychotic' symptoms.

Sutton runs the Winnicott clinic in a very deprived area in Manchester. The landscape is bad schools, dangerous streets, run-down inner-city estates, single mothers, poverty, racism. Few reasons to be cheerful, Sutton knows. But he argues passionately that bad is getting worse. Sutton claims that schools, as well as families, are no longer safe. Teachers who once could provide authority and security, qualities that every single psychiatrist insists a child needs, have been rubbished since the 1980s.

'Children don't feel safe out there,' Sutton told me.

Safety is a good word. Parents are there to make children feel safe, to provide that bedrock security. You explore the world and come home to mum and dad.

Parents need to provide safety and a stress-free zone. Mrs Thatcher once said that family was the one place where there was no bargaining. She was criticised for being naive. It may be a rare example of the Iron Lady being idealistic. All too often, families are riddled with bargaining and competition.

Stress and the child

What can you do if you can see your child is under stress?

The most basic rule is to talk, to make your child feel loved and to make her or him feel you can be trusted so they can confide in you.

Key areas to probe include:

- Is he or she being bullied at school?
- Is she or he scared of failing at school?
- Is the worry that you may be going to divorce?
- Is the child worried that he or she is letting you down – and if so why?
- Does one child feel you love another child more?
- Does he or she hate their brother/sister/stepbrother for some reason?
- Is she worried because she may be pregnant?
- Has your child started to take drugs?

Every family will have its own saga. The key point is that the behaviourist John B. Watson was right; children can talk. Fathers and mothers have to get them to talk. It is easier to talk in a crisis if you are a family that talks anyway. Much depends on the age of the child. It is virtually impossible to get an 18-year-old who does not want to talk to confide in you. But a 14-year-old is different – and the younger children are, the easier it is as long as you remember the kind of techniques Ceci recommended. Be patient. Give them time. Do not lose your cool. Do not assume you know what is wrong with them.

Drink and drugs

Some parents will get upset if their children smoke the occasional joint, but hardly worry if they drink 4 pints of lager. According to the Home Office, 50% of under-15s have tried cannabis and 15% have tried ecstasy. The government appears to be softening its line on cannabis which actually can make the situation of parents more difficult.

Trying to escape and, therefore, not talk is often central to eating disorders and addiction. Both are a withdrawal from life, a withdrawal from the family – and especially upsetting for parents. There are moral and medical issues. Morally, I have no real problem with cannabis. I never had any issue with my children smoking small amounts of it – even regularly. Crack, cocaine and heroin are different. I worry especially because many teenagers put on the bravado of being a narcotics expert who can tell good score from bad; in fact, research consistently shows that the 'quality' of drugs sold on the street is poor. Drugs are mixed with all kinds of poisons and strange substances. In a black market, the buyer can hardly complain if he gets second-rate heroin.

Occasional use is one thing; addiction is very different. I don't think it makes much difference whether a child is addicted to cannabis, cocaine, heroin or alcohol. Alcohol acts as a powerful depressant on many teenagers. Child and teenage drinking is rising in all Western countries. 33% of American school children in grade 12 say they have been drunk at least once in the previous 30 days

(1998 figures, Century Council). Alcohol Concern in the UK say 33% of 11–15-year-olds drink regularly.

The first problem for parents is to know just what is going on. This is not easy because most children and teenagers who drink or take drugs do their best to hide it from their parents. You have to watch for:

- changes in personality;
- excessive moodiness;
- rudeness;
- mood swings.

If you think your child is drinking alone in his or her bedroom, try to ask about it. Don't confront but don't ignore – a balance that is not easy to achieve. It is never easy to coax a surly, secretive teenager out of the bedroom, but it can be done. Do not, as I have known parents do, just lose your temper and say things like 'if you ever do that again I'll throw you out of the house.' Teenagers do sometimes leave home for good after such rows.

There are no simple answers if your child has a drink or drugs problem. Miles Davis was hooked on heroin for years, but, after the death of one of his friends, he went home to his father's house. His father said all he could do to help was to give him a flat in his house. Davis went in there, locked himself away for 10 days, suffered all the pains of withdrawal and somehow kicked the habit. When he came out, he said he and his father smiled at each other as they had not done for years.

Studies of addiction suggest that people can only change when they want to change. Arguing, tough love, logic have no effect. I have known relatives and friends who have nearly died of heroin overdoses, who have vomited on my living-room carpet, who passed out in an alcoholic stupor. The best you can do as a parent is to be there, to nag, to humour and to hope that the moment will come when the addict is so angry she or he becomes motivated to do something about it. The chances are it won't work the first time around. But, often, it eventually will work. Miles Davis is one of thousands who do conquer addiction.

Eating disorders

The National Institute for Eating Disorders claim that every day in the UK some 60,000 people are suffering from some sort of eating disorder – either anorexia or bulimia. There are fierce controversies about causes – depression, the refusal to fit the shape men want and to delay becoming a sexual being. Susie Orbach in *Fat is a Feminist Issue* argued low self-esteem was a cause too. In a celebrity-crazed society, where you can't afford to look bad, boys are starting to suffer from such diseases in considerable numbers too.

If your child is suffering from anorexia or bulimia you need to get professional help as soon as possible. In America there is a heated debate about the numbers of deaths from eating disorders. The pessimists claim 15,000 annual deaths, the optimists a mere 950. Whatever the true statistics, the problem is serious. Still, there are thousands of girls and boys who get over it usually with counselling. Be careful you don't accentuate the problem by nagging a child to eat. Anorexics have strong wills. They use them to stop themselves eating and so they are likely to win a battle of wills even if it is self-destructive. Get help.

Medication

There is also an irony. While we condemn the use of
drugs, more and more children in Britain and America
are being put on medication to deal with mental-health
problems. Psychiatrists like those at Prestwich sometimes
admit that one reason for prescribing medication is that a
young person causes so much anxiety for others. The only
way for others to manage is to sedate him or her. They
argue that child psychiatry is badly resourced with only
about 600 beds in psychiatric units specially designed for
the under-16s. Often, doctors often have no alternative. It
is very difficult to extract figures on how many children
and teenagers under 18 are on medication in the UK.

Just as mothers who are put on antidepressants when
they suffer from postnatal depression often become addicted, children who are put on medication are often condemned to years of side effects and addiction. In a short-
term crisis, medication can help and even save life. But, all
too often, GPs just repeat prescriptions because 'everyone' is frightened of the child being out of control if she or
he is taken off drugs.

Be careful before you consent to your child going on
medication. Always talk to your child. She or he has
rights. If necessary, consult an organisation like MIND.
Always ask for a second opinion.

The attraction/distraction of guilt

Guilt is a perennial problem when things go wrong. But
guilt does not usually help. If you are inclined to blame
yourself, a book is unlikely to stop you doing that. But I

hope you ask yourself why you feel that way and how to change. Guilt often makes bad situations worse; those who suffer from it can become resentful and 'passive aggressive'.

Giles (not his real name) is a barrister. He said:

we didn't pretend. I was very shocked when I discovered my daughter had been bunking off school ... worried for her and guilty that I didn't know. My mother who really should have known better to some extent colluded but ... I then knew my daughter was taking drugs and that she was drinking far too much. I was never sure whether to confront her or to collude. I would give her money and she would spend it on drink and drugs which didn't make her feel any better. She could be charming but she was often very cut off. I didn't shut my eyes but all I could do was tell her I was there ... It did not feel good at the time. I was scared. When she went out, I often caught myself waiting listening till I heard the door banging and she was back home.

In all these difficult situations, fathers need to discover a balance between reasonable worry and panic. A parent who never worries will ignore danger signs and may well be indifferent. A parent who panics will risk making a difficult situation worse. There are no easy answers if your child is very sick. You need to keep battling with energy, hope, common sense and love.

After many attempts, Giles's daughter stopped drinking. She has lost a stone and feels better about herself. Giles is still given to being overanxious and she accuses him sometimes of acting as if she were 12 not 18. He doesn't find it easy to stop worrying, though he knows that may make it harder for her to grow up and grow away from him. They were, when I last talked to them, struggling with these complex issues.

Physical problems

Serious physical problems need specialist medical help. At the end of the book, I list specialist organisations that offer advice and counselling to parents. You will also need a good relationship with your GP. Sadly, many GPs feel too stressed to give patients the time to talk about complex problems. (GPs often say that the fact that they can't talk stresses them even more!) Many patients still feel they cannot complain about them and so accept second-rate treatment that they never would from a garage.

If you feel you are being fobbed off, under NHS provisions, you can get a second opinion and you can complain. As important, you can try to find an organisation that has specialist knowledge and experience of your child's problem. Many of these are self-help groups. Self-help groups are sometimes opinionated, but you can at least discuss your situation with people who have direct personal experience of what you are trying to cope with.

Relationship carry-on

In *Coming up for Air,* Orwell described a typical middle-class marriage in the 1930s. The wife was obsessed with saving money; the husband lied to her all the time. No real contact, no communication, no joy.

Today, our expectations are higher. Your spouse or partner has to be your friend, your Tantric-Fantastic lover, your partner. There's only a point in permanence if you're 32 times happier, better adjusted, more integrated, on top of your narcissism and tendency to drink too many Tequila Sunrises, than you would be if you were single.

And then come the kids.

Children change a relationship. Having a child is one of the most stressful events according to the Life Events scale. It radically alters your sense of yourself. It binds you to someone else even if you split up later.

One of the reforms promised by the Blair government in 2001 is that mothers will now be entitled to 26 weeks paid maternity leave. This reform, however, does nothing for fathers, nothing for the relationship between couples and only guarantees women will be even more responsible for childcare. Surveys show that even when a couple has 'progressive ideals', and have so far shared housecare to allow both to concentrate on their careers, a baby tends to plunge them back into a more traditional division. The woman stays at home; the man becomes the breadwinner. The result is often anger and resentment. Any couple that lives together can find hundreds of reasons for blaming each other. Never underestimate that human capacity for blame.

I have been a champion at blaming and being blamed. Who changes the nappies? Who makes sure the baby has clean clothes? Who gets up in the middle of the night when she's howling? You never lift a borging finger. And you spend all the money down the pub, at the betting shop, on your bloody clothes. Sometimes, the rows are much more serious. Feminist writers have pointed out that many women lose years out of their careers because they are stuck with the childcare, the whole childcare and nothing but the childcare. Superwoman may manage to cook, look after the kids and operate at the level she worked at before she had children, but why should women be forced to be superwomen?

It's not easy to learn how to preserve your relationship while taking good care of your new baby. The theory is simple. You mustn't lose sight of what first drew you to each other. Stressed women, busy men, don't find it easy to make the space, time and bubble in which you can be together as a couple again. You can't just nip out to have an Indian, talk it through and come back and bury your row away.

I remember endlessly ringing Aileen to explain why I was coming home late. The trains were late; the traffic was terrible; I had to rush and do an interview on which the fate of the world depended. I thought my ringing showed that I hadn't forgotten her. Her view was different. I was trying to make myself feel better. Today, mobile phones make constant dysfunctional couple communication possible. I suspect that soon someone will write a PhD on mobile phones and marital dis-satisfaction.

Marital satisfaction

The statistics on so-called 'marital satisfaction' after a baby is born are contradictory. On the one hand, having children tends to protect a marriage. Couples are less likely to split up if they have a child – and they are much less likely to split up in the first year after the birth of a child. On the other hand, for the last 25 years, having children has been seen as one of the main causes of stress in relationships. A study in 1986 found that in the year after a child was born, the so-called 'level of marital satisfaction' changed.

The psychologists compared how couples saw the relationship at three points – when they both knew a baby was on the way, when the baby was born and when their child was 1 year old. Obviously, the experiences of couples were very different. Some were so happy to be parents nothing else mattered. But sheer delight was rarer than the happy-families myth might suggest.

Some 60% of couples reported no change in marital satisfaction. A small number said they felt happier but, generally, the trend was down. A quarter felt somewhat less satisfied; in 10% of the sample, having a baby triggered deep-seated marital dissatisfaction. The reasons were often complex. First, both mother and father tended to feel tired. The men often felt that they were being neglected. The mother was more in love with the baby than with them. The mothers were often resentful.

Their life had become far narrower. One woman referred
to it as 'the home prison'. A woman who feels incarcerated
in the home prison isn't her old bubbly self who used to
charm you. The National Childbirth Trust paints a more
positive picture. As I said earlier, however, the 463 'post-
birth' replies were only 53% of the original sample, and
they are likely to have been the men who felt more positive
and involved anyway. The others would have binned the
questionnaire.

Fathers, sons and relationships

One curiosity – having a son seems to disrupt a marriage
more than having a girl but, paradoxically, for men a son
seems to make it harder to leave the marriage. They may
be less happy but they don't leave; many say they have an
obligation to their son.

A small 1997 National Childbirth Trust study showed
that 33% of men reported a real decline in their sex life; the
larger 2000 survey found over 50% of men said they had
less sex usually because of tiredness. A recent study at the
University of Minnesota found that 40% of women did not
welcome sex 3 months after childbirth because of pain
during intercourse. Miles (1994) argues that for many
women there is a shift of priorities, and that 'what used
to be their sex life can now become his appetite alone.' She
points out that a woman who has had just 5 hours sleep
and who is dreading the baby starting to yelp at 2 a.m. is
hardly likely to 'welcome her husband's advances with
yelps of joy and open arms and legs.'

But, as Miles herself suggests, the reasons may be
more complex. There are obvious reasons – intercourse

can hurt after childbirth – and there are less easy to understand reasons.

Parents and paranoia

George and Jeanette (not their real names) used to make love many mornings but, once they had a baby, it was very different. First of all, one of them had often been up at 3 a.m. to feed the baby. So one partner was exhausted even if the other one was randy. It felt as if the baby was crying and had to be changed all the time. Sex was the last thing on Jeanette's mind. George was frustrated and Jeanette was angry. She was angry because he made it clear he was frustrated. She was also angry because she was anxious because of their history. He expected his weekly nookie. Jeanette began to worry that he might be flirting or sleeping with someone at the office, she told me.

She became so angry at herself for worrying about it that their sex life stopped totally. They would sleep, not touching, in the same bed. When he tried to make love to her, she just rebuffed him. It pleased her because she had power over him. But it took her years to admit that to herself, she told me.

Sometimes, men have strange responses too. Jack McHarris (not his real name) lives in Liverpool. He teaches at one of the local universities. He was pleased to be a father again but surprised that it seemed to destroy his sex drive or, at least, his physical desire for his wife. 'I just did not find her desirable at all. I mean I've no idea if she'd gone off me as well because I really just stopped fancying her.'

Two years on, McHarris and his wife have separated. She now lives deep in the Yorkshire moors while he has returned to Aberdeen. He still feels both guilty and a little baffled about his sudden lack of desire. He still found her beautiful but she aroused absolutely no desire.

Both these couples were unable to talk honestly about their feelings.

In his great play *Cat on a Hot Tin Roof*, Tennessee Williams makes one of his characters, Big Daddy, say that when a marriage starts to go wrong, it starts to go wrong in bed. Talking about sex, negotiating about sex is hard partly because sex is meant to be romantic, spontaneous, magical. It's not like talking about whether you paint the skirting green or white. It's also embarrassing because, when a couple has to talk about their sex life they almost certainly aren't having much of one. Or much of one together.

Miles almost seems to approve of mothers who become uninterested in sex with the fathers of their children. The man's done his job. Can't expect any more of the sperm producer. Concentrate on the children. Since Miles is interested in psychotherapy, I can't help fantasising about one of these 'no sex please I'm a mother now' mothers explaining to her kids ten years later: 'Oh I stopped having a sex life, kiddo, when you were born. I was really glad ... It was what I really wanted all along ... a chance to be frigid ... and frustrate your dad.'

Excuse me, I have to snore

I remember coming home from work when Nicholas was 4 months old. Aileen was already annoyed because she felt she had no time and energy to write. She had started an

MPhil but was on the verge of giving it up. Meanwhile, I had my first big break as a film director.

As I walked in, Aileen handed me our son. She was furious and half in tears. She was dog-tired, he had been crying all day, she had been trying to comfort him all day. She just couldn't take it any more. She had to sleep.

I was exhausted myself. I was making *Anatomy of a Pin Up*, a short about the Penthouse Organisation. The executive producer Walter Shenson had produced the Beatles films. I was desperate to impress. I was juggling with a neurotic junior producer, a prima donna camera-man, the politics of the Penthouse Organisation and nude models. The models had a problem relevant to this book. They worried how their fathers would feel if they saw them nude on the news-stands.

I was in no mood to take the baby. I couldn't believe what was happening. Still, I took the baby and Aileen went to sleep. In the morning, I was off on location again. I expected gratitude which, of course, I didn't get. She was furious I was off again, ignoring the fact that she had another day in the 'home prison', and that I was sure to be late again.

Aileen's mother was so worried by the tone of her letters she flew in on a rescue mission from America to help us cope.

I am ashamed to say I was not the most loving, atten-tive or sensitive husband after our first son was born. It was only when the children were much older that I was able to hear how isolated and cut-off Aileen felt at the time, and how my behaviour was not helping. We both paid for it. Aileen can still get very angry with me, but we also failed as a couple to talk about the crises at the time. We did not admit how competitive we were with each other. For young couples, men and women in their 20s especially as we were, it often remains difficult to say this is what I need without it turning into a fight.

Miles pokes fun at one man who was finally driven to beg 'but I only want ten minutes of your time.' Miles is right in saying men have no right to expect sex from their wives or partners. You have to be Mr Hardon Crass to get truly fed up if your wife does not want to make love 3 or 4 months after she has given birth. But, what if it doesn't change? After 6 months, maybe it's reasonable to be worried and, at least, to want to talk about it properly. Miles seems to suggest that if a man wants to do that it's oppressive.

I don't approve of Miles' disapproval. It seems to me she comes close to recommending women use the power becoming a mother gives them to become totally manipulative and to use that power to withhold sex. The French say one person kisses, the other one permits the kiss. One person wants: the other is wanted. It always needs courage to raise questions of desire, of how often it is normal to have sex. You can't be sure what you will hear. It may be that she has stopped fancying you; it may be he has a lover. It's bound to be difficult, but if you don't do it what will happen to the relationship? People do not put up with cold 1930s marriages easily these days.

How to talk about sex deserves a book all of its own. I suggest a few basics and I know these are counsels of perfection and that perfection, is hard to achieve when you are unlaid and feel unloved. But try. Listen more than you complain. Try not to get angry or resentful. Try to understand how she or he feels. Try to agree things you can do which will take some of the bitterness out of the situation.

But sex is not the only source of friction – pun intended, writer's brain has not gone into coma. Based on extensive research, I have compiled a list of typical arguments that couples have in the year after the birth of child (Box 11).

Box 11   Typical arguments

- arguments about time – you can go out; I am stuck in the home prison;
- arguments about housework – you never do anything;
- arguments about shopping;
- arguments about money – you waste our money down the pub;
- arguments about sharing parenting – you never get up at night to give him the bottle;
- arguments about ignoring the other person – I might as well not be here;
- arguments about your parents – you think your mum knows more about the baby than I do;
- arguments about the relationship in general – we don't talk any more;
- arguments about desire – you just don't fancy me any more;
- arguments about sex – we don't make love any more or making love has become very boring;
- arguments about the other children and how they respond to the baby.
- Every couple will have its own quirky flash-points.

Research on conflict resolution and mediation in divorce shows that, often, couples are so angry and disappointed, they blame each other for everything that has gone wrong. It sounds preachy but the only way through couple problems is to talk about them, say how you feel, listen to how the other person feels and compromise and change. There is no hard evidence to suggest that men are worse at doing this or are more stubborn than women.

Carry on couple – of clematis and clitoris

So much of our literature is about conflict and break-up, we forget the old orthodoxies work. The couple carries on. You watch your children grow up. Sex becomes less passionate, more comforting. You probably will never again attempt Tantric Position X. Still there are compensations as, to use William Congreve's marvellous verb, you 'dwindle' into a couple.

There are some things you like doing together, many things you'll do because she likes it and the rules of tit for tat, or clematis and clitoris, operate. If you visit, which she loves, the garden centre (the clematis), she'll go to the cinema to see obscure art movies, you love, even if they're risqué (the clitoris). Not Romeo and Juliet, but then, they died because they failed to communicate adequately about the honeymoon arrangements.

If someone asks you, you can say honestly your marriage or relationship is quite good. You are best friends. You can still manage a bit of sex as long as it's not terribly Tantric. The children are great, wonderful 'fruit of your loins'. They make up for everything and you are no longer very sure what the everything you missed out on is. So you're ready to totter hand in hand into the carbon-clogged sunset.

Still this semi-romantic finale assumes you have got your relationship with your children right, that you see them, talk to them and don't bore them, that next time they come for Sunday lunch they'll want to hear about the obscure art movie and help prune the clematis. This will not happen by magic. Like other relationships, relationships with children need time, work and imagination. But there is a difference. In romantic relationships, success is staying together; with children the good enough parent knows that success is letting go. We have our children as 'ours', to have and look after and enjoy day in, day out, just for a time. Time for them to grow, time for them to grow away, time for them to grow into themselves.

The father who lives just for his children is storing up trouble for himself, and almost certainly, for them too. Often, children come first. But not always, not in every case. Cherish and care, with intelligence and sensitivity, for your other relationships too.

10

The price of being a father

Children are not cheap. It has been calculated that every child will cost his father and mother £75,000 by the time he or she is 18 years old, assuming he or she stays in state education. Parents who send their children to public school now have to pay on average £13,000 a year for boarding and £6,000 for day schools. Pocket money, that invention of the Victorian middle class who wanted to teach their children about thrift, now averages £12.50 a week for middle-class 14-year-olds in London.

By 1939, pocket money was common enough to support a thriving comic industry. In his essay on boys' weeklies, George Orwell describes ten comics, the *Gem*, *Magnet*, *Modern Boy*, *Triumph*, *Champion*, *Wizard*, *Rover*, *Skipper* and *Adventure* that competed just for boy readers. All had large circulations. Orwell criticised these weeklies for peddling public-school snobberies to working-class boys, fantasies which helped perpetuate the class system The weeklies also seem antique because they did not have stories on style and sex, essential knowledge for today's pre-teen. No advice on how to chat girls up, on what clothes to wear or what deodorant the cool teenager should spray. Orwell was writing about the pre-brand universe though, in fact, many of today's prime brands like Coca Cola, Ford, were already household names.

In the 1930s left-wing critics had more serious issues than the power of the brands. Brands had certainly not 'reached out' to children. Today, parents have to deal with children who are aware of brands and advertising from the age of 3. By the age of 6, children know some brands are cool while others are yuck. So today's dad also must be able to discuss – and look up on the Internet – the relative merits of Nike (supercool) and Reebok (yuck, yesterday-ville) as well as the state of Posh and Becks marriage which is often covered in tweenie-girl mags.

Two huge cinema hits – *Superman* in 1977 and *Star Wars* – were landmarks in opening up the global children's market. Both films saw merchandising aimed at children on a scale not seen before in Britain. Sales of Superman dolls, Darth Vader dolls, light sabres, Obi-Wan Kenobi dolls made billions more than the films took at the box office.

Soon after *Star Wars*, too, the first personal computers came on the market. I want to suggest this has had unexpected social consequences. Throughout history, parents have given and children, while they were young, have had nothing concrete to give in return other than the joy they give. Joy don't pay the bills. Today, it's different and we're seeing a shift not in economic – but in knowledge-based power. Children are often more at home with computers than their parents. It is the first time that children are better than their fathers at a task of real practical value.

You want to set up your bank account on line? Well actually you have to ask your 10-year-old to do it and he only will if you agree to get him a Playstation for Xmas.

Playstation is a good example of a brand that has become a must-have for many children.

I recommend, when this shift of power depresses, you sing to the tune of 'Some of my Favourite Things' from *The Sound of Music* my specially adapted lyric:

> *Pepsi and Nike and McDonalds*
> *these are a few of my favourite brands*
> *when the bee stings*
> *when the bills bite*
> *when I'm feeling sad*
> *I simply remember my favourite brands*
> *and then I don't feel so bad …*

At least it will embarrass your children.

Marketing to kids and stress

Worldwide, the so-called child market is reported to be worth $64 billion – far more than the GDP of virtually every country in Africa. There are learned journals devoted to selling to kids and a booming conference circuit where gurus offer workshops on 'what works with kids and why', 'peer group marketing', 'research methods for all your needs' and advice on how to 'think like a kid'. 'There's a conference every day on marketing to kids and if advertisers really knew how to sell to children, they wouldn't be doing that,' Jeffrey Goldstein, professor of psychology at the University of Utrecht, told me.

Consultancies like The Brand Works for Kids and Focus on Kids reveal how to build 'a wall of communication' to influence 'your core consumer lifestyle' from the moment said consumer is 2 years old. The unspoken aim is to turn kids into avid consumers.

In Sweden, the government has banned all advertising during children's TV in order to protect youngsters from being unduly influenced. (Is this why, perhaps, the Swedes cannot bear to borg for a society which bans ads for Lego and Pokemon?)

Once it was argued that, until they were 5 years old, children could not tell the difference between advertising and 'normal' T.V programmes. Many psychologists claim children still don't get the commercial motive when they are older, even if they can spot the difference between the advertising 'genre' and programmes. Glen Smith who runs the Children's Research Unit in London disagrees. He claims children who are much younger understand advertising. In one study, he showed commercials to 4-year-olds. 'We had dolls representing children, mum, dad and so on. We asked the children to move the doll the ad was talking to forward. We found if there was a frozen pea commercial they moved the mum forward, if it was a toy they moved the child doll forward.' Proof for Smith that young kids understand who the sales pitch is aimed at.

Many parents don't think you need a research programme to prove that.

Pester power

Many parents report that it is difficult not to feel that they are letting their children down because they simply cannot afford to buy them things. This is perhaps worst at Christmas where the average British family spends over £250 on toys. This is about 50% of what a small family on benefit would get for a whole month.

Even affluent parents get very irritated with being nagged to buy things by their kids. From when they were 3 years old, Hannah and Victoria started to make lists of the toys they wanted for Xmas. 'Victoria had a childminder who had 40 Barbie dolls,' her mother Rowan told me, so Barbies were Victoria's first favourites. And she's passed Barbie-mania on to her sister. Hannah's 4th birthday was a Barbie fest. 'Victoria is now old enough to understand that money is not limitless but Hannah is still too young to have understood that message,' Rowan told me. She minds particularly about toys like Beanie Babies because after a few months they'll stop being used. Unfortunately, Beanie Babies now are Victoria's favourite. 'I sleep with Beanie Babies,' Victoria told me. Rowan and her husband Phil feel that the relentless pressure of advertising causes stress.

One cleric, the Revd Gordon Warren has gone so far as to preach a sermon against Pokemon cards. At the end of it, he tore up the cards in his pulpit. 'It isn't just symbolic some of the people who are spending on this are very poor.' But they feel harassed by their children who want to have what other kids have.

I want to suggest, however, that we should not just see children as defenceless in the brand wars. In 2000 and 2001, I was involved with two projects – the Victoria and Albert's *brand-new* exhibition and the BBC TV series *Shopology* – which suggest today's middle-class kids at least are brand and media literate. I filmed focus groups of children run by advertising agencies. What the children said made it clear that even 7-year-olds are often remarkably savvy about clothes, spending and fashion.

Ten-year-old Harry took part in one of these focus groups. Harry is smart. His favourite brand is Reebok. I put to Harry the claim Coca Cola have often made that a child's room is the same all over the world and that, given children from Rio to Romford have the same needs, a brand like theirs can answer children's deepest emotional needs.

'Rubbish' Harry laughed – and he understood the question just like an adult would.

'But why do you like Reebok?'

He giggled. He didn't know. But it didn't trouble him. His father said that there was peer pressure in the school. It was a point made by other parents. If children have the right brands, they don't stand out and they are less likely to be bullied.

Older teenagers are also obsessed by brands. For my films for the Victoria and Albert, I talked to a group of 15 teenagers from Barking and Dagenham. All had somehow managed to buy, or have bought for them, all manner of designer kit even though most of them came from poor families. A promising athlete, Debbie wears nothing but Nike, Nike trainers, Nike top, Nike cap. If Nike did knickers, Debbie would have them. This mainly working-class group was far less analytical than the middle-class kids the advertising agencies used in the focus groups I filmed.

Children, advertising

The paradox is that research shows that children are sceptical about advertising – and that is particularly true of girls. Merris Griffiths of Aberystwyth University showed TV ads to primary-school children in Wales. When they view ads for dolls and other toys, 7-year-old girls 'respond with surprising hostility. You'd think none of them had ever played with a Barbie doll,' Griffiths told me. The older children are not just knowing but dismissive. 'I started showing groups of 7–11-year-olds ten selected ads for toys,' Griffiths told me. In all, she used ten ads – three for girls' toys, three for boys' and four neutral ones.

The children rejected the ads. Griffiths added, 'They felt insulted by them. The girls had the most hostile reactions. They were totally cynical.' This was as true of the 7-year-old girls as of the 11-year-old girls. 'They'd say things like this is trickery,' she said. The extent of the cynicism surprised her.

Media consultants take for granted the critical awareness of today's children. Nicky Buss of the advertising agency Ammirati Puris Lintas reports 7-year-old watching the Burger King Lost Worlds ad using glove puppets. One carped; 'Why is that man got his hand up a sock. Don't they know how to do it properly? That's not going to get me to buy it is it?'

The advertisers are fighting back, however. Focus on Kids, for example, suggest 32 different techniques for marketing to children and recommend 'building a motivating promotional mechanic' to link up with a charity. Some 67% of children are 'more predisposed' to your product if you do.

Griffiths argues advertisers now use special techniques on television to counter the knowingness of children. A content analysis of 20 TV ads showed the ads are 'gendered'; subtle techniques are used to appeal to boys or girls. Ads for boys' toys use far more high angle shots – emphasising their superiority. Ads for girls' toys use far more low angle shots. Ads for boys' toys are paced faster and use cuts far more than dissolves.

These techniques – especially the prevalence of cuts over dissolves – may not sound sinister but, Professor John Murray of Kansas State University thinks otherwise. Murray was part of 1992 American Psychological Association Task working party on children and television. On mainstream television, Murray told me:

*'the time for children's programmes is quite limited
so ads have to appeal to a wide age group. The
problem with children's programmes is that most
are aimed at a very broad age group – around 2
to 12. There's only one way you can keep the attention of both - and 12-year-olds and that is to have
very fast-paced fast-action programmes.'*

Murray has done content analysis on American programmes on Saturday mornings, a key period for children. Most are cartoons with fast cuts and fast action.
The easiest way of achieving fast pace is violence,
Murray said. The average number of violent events in
an hour of children's television includes 24 deaths as
opposed to 5 deaths per hour on prime-time adult TV.

'Laughter goes along with many of these deaths – and
I just can't think that's good.' Murray predicted pressure
in the wake of the Columbine school shootings to curb
violence in programmes and ads.

Griffiths' findings also made her worry about violence.
The Welsh children enjoyed car ads much more than toy
ads. 'They seemed to treat them more as light entertainment than as advertising.' Griffiths was struck by how
most of her subjects responded to an ad for the Citroen
Saxo. This ad has animation where the strong Saxo sur-
vives being rammed, booted and attacked. The violence is
funny. But what impressed Griffiths was 'how much the
children loved it.'

James Aitchison of the Advertising Association dis-
missed concerns about violence and denied anything im-
proper. He said Murray was working up moral panics.
'The debate on violence and television has been going
on for years and is totally inconclusive,' Aitchison said.

The media-literate child can also spot some crucial
messages that make an ad an ad. Brian Young, professor

of psychology at Exeter University, showed 66 children aged 4–8 years two sorts of ad – the genuine article and doctored ads. The doctored ads had unusual punchlines. One ad showed a face cream. The genuine version extolled a face cream with the punchline that it made you better looking; the doctored version praised the cream but the punchline was it gave you disgusting spots.

Children aged 4–5 years liked the funny endings better and didn't notice whether or not the punchlines made commercial sense. The reactions of 6-year-olds were different. Just over 50% understood there was something wrong with the funny endings but often couldn't say what; just under half responded like the younger kids.

All the 8-year-olds were totally familiar with the advertising game. They laughed at the doctored ads – not just because they were funny but because they were pathetic as ads. A face cream that gives you spots is not a product you'll sell, they pointed out.

And children can be so aware of what sells that advertising agencies use focus groups to get ideas for new products.

Eat my shorts – the creativity of children in relation to brands

The children in one focus group were asked to design a new cereal. A group of 10–12-year-olds came up with the name Eat My Shorts based on Bart Simpson's well-known quip. The packaging would be in the shape of shorts. The kids discussed the royalties they would have to pay to the creators of the Simpsons. They also liked the idea of inserting various add-ons in the package so you would sprinkle chocolate flakes, for example, on the basic cereal. This idea of 'fusion' excited the advertising agency tremendously because they could feed it back to clients who would use it to inspire product development. It would show their clients they knew the yoof market.

Brian Young has found one curious connection between how children see advertising and their personal skills, especially how children understand the need to assert themselves and sometimes show off. 'A number of studies,' Young told me, 'show it's only round the age of 7 that children get a sense of promoting themselves. For example, if you ask 6-year-olds to put themselves, forward to become one of a team they tell you about themselves warts and all.' The 6-year-olds don't understand the presentation of self.

Only round 7 do children understand that if they want to convince others to have them on their team, they need to accentuate the positive and eliminate the negative in the best tradition of 'how to succeed in life' books. Given the evidence that children are growing up younger and have psychological insights that would baffle Piaget, this is a bit surprising but Young insists the findings are robust.

This research suggests one troubling trend, troubling for advertisers at least. Almost as soon as children understand what advertising is about, they become hostile to it. Paradoxically, this hostility doesn't seem to stop them enjoying the ads. Nor, sadly, does it stop them spending money stupidly.

For many fathers, the teenage phone bill will be a concern. I reproduce on the page opposite the alarming document known as my phone bill. Such exhibits often show that more was spent on the Internet including sites such as Porn o Vision and Blondes in Baluchistan than on sober phone calls to research this book. If ever there was a subject which requires the talk-to-your-children approach this is it.

Your Customer No.   LN 2629 7516 Q011
Date (and tax point)   8 August 2001

Breakdown of information for (020) 7987 2827   Page 4 of 5

Other calls over £0.40 (itemised) - continued

Date	Time	Destination		Duration (hrs:mins:secs)	Cost before discount (£)
1 Jun	19:27	Mobile Phone	07949 209138	0:06:26	0.903
4 Jun	17:37	Mobile Phone	07949 209138	0:04:09	0.817
4 Jun	22:23	Mobile Phone	07803 708648	0:38:45	6.079
5 Jun	10:16	Mobile Phone	07810 013667	0:02:23	0.405
5 Jun	19:27	Mobile Phone	07803 708648	0:10:41	1.675
5 Jun	22:53	Mobile Phone	07803 708648	0:20:13	3.172
6 Jun	18:10	Mobile Phone	07956 891977	0:08:27	1.187
12 Jun	08:38	Mobile Phone	07803 708648	0:12:32	2.025
12 Jun	19:39	Mobile Phone	07803 708648	0:21:02	3.299
12 Jun	21:59	Mobile Phone	07803 708648	0:03:33	0.557
12 Jun	23:17	Mobile Phone	07803 708648	0:32:01	5.023
13 Jun	19:23	Mobile Phone	07803 708648	0:15:04	2.363
13 Jun	23:06	Mobile Phone	07803 708648	0:06:13	0.974
15 Jun	13:14	Mobile Phone	07779 168633	0:05:22	0.997
18 Jun	22:19	Mobile Phone	07803 708648	0:02:54	0.453
18 Jun	22:25	Mobile Phone	07803 708648	0:05:08	0.805
19 Jun	18:12	Mobile Phone	07803 708648	0:03:08	0.491
19 Jun	20:58	Mobile Phone	07803 708648	0:10:32	1.651
19 Jun	23:25	Mobile Phone	07803 708648	0:29:56	4.697
20 Jun	18:39	Mobile Phone	07803 708648	0:06:04	0.952
20 Jun	21:06	Mobile Phone	07803 708648	0:02:50	0.443
21 Jun	20:19	Mobile Phone	07803 708648	0:07:10	1.123
21 Jun	22:55	Mobile Phone	07803 708648	0:15:19	2.402
24 Jun	18:11	Mobile Phone	07765 007923	0:08:38	0.544
24 Jun	18:27	Mobile Phone	07989 560305	0:18:21	1.089
25 Jun	22:56	Mobile Phone	07803 708648	0:20:30	3.26
26 Jun	18:58	Mobile Phone	07803 708648	0:05:54	0.925
26 Jun	20:23	Mobile Phone	07803 708648	0:08:16	1.296
26 Jun	22:55	Mobile Phone	07803 708648	0:11:28	1.797
26 Jun	23:13	Mobile Phone	07803 708648	0:16:49	2.637
27 Jun	19:29	Mobile Phone	07803 708648	0:06:48	1.065
27 Jun	23:13	Mobile Phone	07803 708648	0:06:02	0.945
2 Jul	17:01	Mobile Phone	07810 430132	0:25:46	4.376
3 Jul	23:38	Mobile Phone	07803 708648	0:21:24	3.357
4 Jul	01:13	Mobile Phone	07803 708648	0:08:35	1.345
4 Jul	23:30	Mobile Phone	07803 708648	0:26:23	4.139
5 Jul	21:04	Mobile Phone	07803 708648	0:16:31	2.592
5 Jul	23:16	Mobile Phone	07803 708648	0:09:31	1.492
6 Jul	18:58	Mobile Phone	07803 708648	0:02:34	0.402
9 Jul	09:25	Mobile Phone	07803 708648	0:05:19	0.859
9 Jul	12:31	Mobile Phone	07939 625786	0:02:25	0.473
9 Jul	22:37	Mobile Phone	07803 708648	0:15:17	2.396
10 Jul	23:24	Mobile Phone	07803 708648	0:14:55	2.339
10 Jul	23:56	Mobile Phone	07803 708648	0:02:35	0.404
11 Jul	20:14	Mobile Phone	07803 708648	0:11:31	1.807
11 Jul	21:17	Mobile Phone	07803 708648	0:14:15	2.235
11 Jul	22:03	Mobile Phone	07941 867804	0:03:41	0.517
12 Jul	20:21	Mobile Phone	07803 708648	0:03:10	0.496
12 Jul	20:25	Mobile Phone	07803 708648	0:08:53	1.394
12 Jul	23:12	Mobile Phone	07803 708648	0:08:03	1.263
13 Jul	10:08	Mobile Phone	07977 202191	0:03:28	0.639
13 Jul	13:10	Mobile Phone	07941 867804	0:05:11	1.02
14 Jul	19:09	Mobile Phone	07721 005977	0:07:12	0.454
14 Jul	19:30	Mobile Phone	07775 816161	0:13:28	0.848
15 Jul	23:53	Mobile Phone	07803 708648	0:18:13	1.983

In Chapter 11, I show, incidentally, that by the time they are teenagers children have usually lost any diffidence about lying when it comes to money, boyfriends and girl-friends.

Everything I have written so far applies in some way to fathers and children from birth to the starts of the teens. In Chapters 11 and 12, I look at the relationship between fathers and children when they get older. If Dreikurs spoke of a power struggle when the children are young, the power struggle now gets worse – seriously worse.

11

Teenage traumas

The emperor penguin warms the egg between his feet for months, we saw. But, by the time nipper penguin is 2, he has left home. Papa penguin doesn't have to pay his phone bills or fret about his exam results. The human father is in for the long term, however. Biologists argue human childhood lasts so long because we have so much to learn before we are adult and can play our part in society. It's during the teens that we strut on the life stage for the first time and try out different personas:

> *The younger person in order to experience wholeness must feel a progressive continuity between that which he has been during the long years of childhood and that which he promises to become in the anticipated future.*
>
> Erik Erikson

Erikson is a psychoanalyst who has studied adolescence in some depth – and many of the issues he raised 40 years ago are still relevant. By the end of the teens, a young person should have a good sense of who they are, what their values are and what direction their life will take.

Erikson was not particularly interested in the parents' point of view. I want to suggest that from a father's point of view the teens are about being there when you're needed and staying in your box well out of it when you're not. The trouble is who decides when you are needed. Your view of that will be very different from your teenage son or daughter.

Problems of puberty

In Freud's day, the latency period lasted till the start of the teens. Now children become sexual beings much younger than they used to. Girls start to develop breasts somewhere between 8 and 9; many girls start to grow pubic hair when they are 9 years old. The average age for the first period is 12–13 as against 15–16 in the 1850s. We have better hygiene and nutrition to thank, experts say. This means there are now grandmothers in their mid-30s, girls who gave birth when they were 16 and whose daughters also gave birth when they were 16. Some fathers find this pace of development quite hard to deal with as their daughter becomes a sexually mature woman well before she is 13.

Boys go into puberty later than girls but they too are doing so younger than a century ago. Very few boys are not capable of fathering children by the time they are 14. Boys sometimes suffer from a condition known as precocious puberty and develop adult sexual characteristics before they are 10. Fortunately, this condition is very rare as it nearly always is accompanied by serious psychiatric symptoms.

The 1994 study *Sex and America's Teenagers* found that 53% of boys had had intercourse by their 18th birthday as opposed to 26% in the 1960s (see also Hine, 1999). It also found that 54% of girls lost their virginity by the age of 18 as against 23% in the 1960s. But studies also show that 52% of both boys and girs today have only one sexual partner between the ages of 18 and 24 and 11% of both sexes have no partner at all.

But adolescence is not just about sex. Hormonal changes also lead to growth spurts, facial hair, acne; in boys the voice breaks. Teenagers sometimes feel they don't know what their body is going to do next. Much research finds that children in their teens are dissatisfied with their bodies and see themselves not just as ugly but abnormal. In the Netherlands, there now is a vogue for plastic surgery for children and teens. Many teenagers opt for it because they are so self-conscious about their physical appearance. Yet, as ever, there are individual differences. Some 13-year-old girls take pride in having large breasts; others find it embarrassing and hate the stares. The market for anti-acne products is huge – and boys worry about spots and pimples as much as girls. Parents have to learn to be sensitive and, of course, for the following dialogue:

Parent: *I think you look nice.*

Teen: *What do you know? Who cares what you think?*

This teenager has not attained Piaget's logical perfection. I failed to attain logical perfection myself so I shaved off one of my pimples when I was 14 to stop looking like Frankenstein's cousin. I also became convinced I was

going bald which eventually taught me the kind of philosophical lesson Piaget held dear.

How to be a teenager according to masterpieces

The teenager is a modern phenomenon, we think, very
much post-Second World War. The first – and great –
book to catch their energy and rebellion was J. D.
Salinger's *The Catcher in the Rye*. Holden Caufield, the
hero, is cool, anti his parents, anti his school. *Adrian
Mole's Secret Diary* is not in the Salinger class but he
did catch many of the teen neuroses of the 1980s.
Adrian frets about his pimples, his hair, his growth
spurt, the elusive Pandora and, of course, the size of his
thing. His parents appall him because they have zero cool.
The ultimate lows are when his parents don't act their age
and insist on having sex and wearing trendy clothes.

But there's nothing 20th century about 'teens'. The
word was used as early as 1611, according to the *Oxford
Dictionary*; it then meant 'to anger, vex or cause to grieve'.
By 1673, teenager meant someone aged between 13 and
19. Teenage tantrums aren't that 20th century either. One
of my favourite late 19th century novels is *Diary of a
Nobody*. Mr Pooter, the nobody, has to cope with his
18-year-old son. Son Loomis has trouble with girls,
trouble with money and trouble with his get-rich-quick
schemes. When they go wrong, Loomis is good at butter-
ing up mum and sponging off dad. When Pooter finally
gets him a job at the bank where he works, Loomis lets
him down. He makes mistakes, is rude to the bosses and
bunks off.

George didn't identify himself, however, as part of a social group that rejects his father's generation values. Teens as rebels only took hold in the 1950s, according to *Teenagers, an American history* by Grace Palladino (1994). She notes it was that generation of teens who grew up with their fathers away fighting. No dad, no authority perhaps. No one has done enough research to prove the thesis but it would be interesting to look at 'the birth of the teens' in countries like Brazil where men did not have to go to fight the war.

Erik Erikson

Throughout this book, I've warned fathers against being overanxious. This is never truer than in the teens. Fathers of teenagers will have every chance to be over anxious. Many parents say they dread the teens because they expect endless battles (Herbert, 1987) – battles about school, dresses, money, sex, telephone bills, how late you can stay out and being left alone. At the heart of all these issues are questions of control and privacy. How much do you, as a parent, have the right to know about your children? Parents usually think children belong to them and so they have total rights. When children are 8 years old that is totally true; when young people are 20 years old, it's obviously false. At what point does protecting your children become oppressing your children? Fathers need to think about it because many parents hate not knowing everything about their children.

Adolescents should have secrets from their mothers and fathers.

Erik Erikson argued adolescence was a turning point. Erikson had set out the following stages in development.

(I haven't given you these before because, with Piaget's stages and with Freud's stages, you might get to the stage of being totally fed up with stages.) But Erikson's stage theory does help make sense of some of the conflicts teenagers face in themselves and with their parents:

- the baby – basic trust versus mistrust;
- toddlerhood autonomy versus shame;
- early childhood initiative versus guilt;
- later childhood inferiority versus industry;
- identity versus role-confusion adolescence.

These are the basic choices at each stage. Erikson does not argue that babies 'choose'. It's a question of their heredity and their environment, of what parents deal to them. As a therapist, Erikson saw many individuals who gave in to their lot and many others who fought and struggled against all odds. Fates are not fixed. Erikson saw life as a series of challenges. By the end of the teens, young people should have made certain key decisions about themselves – are they heterosexual, what will they do, how do they feel about their future, what are their aims in life. In making these choices, teenagers often tried out various identities and roles.

Parents can't make these choices for their children though they are endlessly tempted to.

Teenagers and toddlers

I want to suggest a possibly outrageous comparison. We've seen how toddlers switch in a flash from pretending to be Batman to playing show-and-tell in the Wendy

House. As they play, switch and pretend, toddlers learn – how to co-operate, what the limits of 'decent' behaviour are, what other people's attitudes are and so on. The skills Erikson suggests teenagers learn by trying out various identities are similar. Only, teenagers don't see themselves as playing games, of course. For them, it is serious and they are far more self-conscious about it. One way to define what you are is to make it clear what you are against. If you're not sure just what you are against, you can try out various options to see which feels best for you.

But there's one big difference between the toddler and the teenager. Montaigne noted that parents love little children and their monkey-like 'frolickings' far more than the same children when they are mature. Usually, parents coo and goo when their 3-year-old swirls a black cape round their shoulder, announces 'I'm Matrix Man' and explains what lies at 'infinity and beyond'. How can his little brain be so imaginative, bless it! You don't get the same adoring response if you are a 14-year-old in New Romantic gear who lectures their parents on the virtues of vegan and why they should mothball the Mondeo to fight global warming.

With toddlers, most parents stay in total control. But teenagers can storm out of the house, disappear overnight to their friends and freak you out with worry. Moreover, you have fewer legal rights than you might think. At 16, children become adults for most legal purposes. They can marry without their parents' consent. You have no right to open their mail and listen to their phone conversations. The only right you have is to pay for all the groceries.

I can reveal The European Court of Human Rights has ruled it is a violation for parents to ask 13-year olds certain questions like 'where are you going tonight and how are you getting home?'. In a landmark case, Father X sued his children on the grounds that, since he pays their mobile-phone bills, he is entitled to know the number of their mobile phone so that he can ring them:

> *I can also exclusively reveal that the last paragraph is a joke. Did you realise that, reader?*

Erikson argued that if teenagers did not try out different identities, they faced dangers. He talked about young men and women who were frozen into 'immature personalities'. The boy who decides at 12 that he is going to be an army officer like Daddy, or an accountant like Daddy, may stop growing up psychologically. He may live in the shadow of his parents for ever and never be able to form proper relationships.

Personal photographs

I have among our family photographs a picture of my mother with her parents. My mother must have been in her mid- to late-20s. Her head is resting on her father's shoulder; she's smiling. It's a touching picture of an affectionate daughter. What's disturbing is the space between the two of them, the father–daughter couple and her mother, Teresa, my grandmother. Teresa stares out, not looking at either of them, a woman totally apart from the other two. The physical affection, the head on the shoulder, is all my mother. When I look at that photograph, I'm often touched but I also remember my father often accusing my mother of being too involved with her parents. She could never be a good wife to him, he stormed, because she had never really left home emotionally. She was always Daddy's girl, even years after Daddy died. It was like so many accusations in marriages – true and not true.

Erikson argued it was healthy to end the role confusion, having tried out different identities by the early 20s. Teenagers who were unable to do this, who could not stop trying one thing and then another, were likely to suffer depression later. The ossified immature personality has sound defences. I am what my parents wanted me to be, and that must be good. The teenager who can't choose is more vulnerable but also more creative.

Explaining boundaries

Erikson, and many others, claim that one of the jobs of the good enough parents is to set boundaries. Setting boundaries is important at all ages and stages but perhaps particularly in the teens. But you can't set boundaries arbitrarily. Fathers can no longer just rely on telling kids to just do as I say.

Andrew and Cathy have five children. They talked about having a large family when they got married though neither of them come from one. Andrew is a police officer; Cathy is a senior social work manager. Their oldest daughter is 13. They live in the countryside near north London. 'Emma is very horse oriented these days so we see little of her,' Andrew told me. Andrew and Cathy had recently had to put their foot down. They had been invited to a party by one of Cathy's colleagues. Emma was going out with friends. Andrew and Cathy had no idea that their daughter would change her plans.

In the middle of the party, Emma rang her parents up on their mobile. She didn't want to come home that night. Her plans had changed. She now wanted to spend the night in a field camping with some friends. A little questioning – Andrew is a policeman, after all – revealed that the friends included some slightly older boys. This is precisely the kind of situation parents of teenagers have to face. Andrew and Cathy didn't think that a very good idea. They were worried about some of the boys. They decided to tell their daughter they would be back by 11.30 and they expected to see her home by then. 'We do lead by example,' Andrew said. They didn't mind curtailing their social life to make the point that Emma also had to be in by 11:30.

I asked Andrew if he thought he would behave the same way when Emma was a 15–16-year-old. He said he was not sure.

The negotiation between Emma and her parents is one of thousands that will take place during the teens. At 15 or 16, young people resent such controls usually and evade them by the simple device of not ringing their parents to say plans have changed. In every family, children will have to ask permission about some things. Do you expect your 12-year-old to tell you (i) that they are going out, (ii) where they are going out to, (iii) when they will be back.

Research suggests this failure to communicate causes thousands of rows every day in the UK between mothers, fathers and teens. But why do parents not do more to avoid these rows? In his rather wise book *Living with Teenagers* Martin Herbert (1987) suggests that it is partly expectation. Many parents make things harder precisely because they expect battles. But the evidence suggests that parents may be worrying unnecessarily.

Don't exaggerate the differences?

A series of studies in America in the 1960s and in the UK in the 1970s showed, however, that it is easy to exaggerate conflict between teens and their parents. Coleman reports a 1976 study where teenagers were asked which of the following statements was very true, true, they were uncertain about or was wrong:

- I get on with my father   35% very true   45% true
- I get on with my mother   40% very true   47% true

Teenagers were also asked to say how often they disagreed with their parents. Fights about important issues:

- same-sex friends   often 3%   sometimes   2%
- opposite sex friends   often 2%   sometimes   9%
- dress and hair style   often 11%   sometimes 35%
- bedtime/staying out   often 8%   sometimes 26%
- homework   often 6%   sometimes 18%

On the basis of such figures, Coleman argues we should not believe the conflict between generations is that intense. He cites American research which also plays down the conflicts between teenagers and their parents. There is one slight problem with these studies, however. The studies rely almost entirely on talking to the teenagers. They did not talk to the parents.

Taboo topix

Sex and the American Teenager (1994) reported over 70% of 16-year-olds and 80% of 18-year-olds found out about sex from school and their friends rather than their parents. In some ways, it's surprising that as late as 1994. So many teenagers should be relying on their parents. In most families in Britain, sex is not discussed, especially not between fathers and their daughters, and mothers and their sons. Some evidence suggests that mothers and daughters do find it easier to talk about sex.

Freud only considered the issue of why children have sexual fantasies about their parents; he did not look at the troubling question of whether some fathers become too possessive of their daughters. At a time when there are well-justified concerns about child abuse, this is a potentially explosive subject. But fathers often have to realise that suddenly they are not the most important man in their daughter's life.

When fathers complain their daughters wear too much make up and too few clothes, daughters fight back and insist they'll stay out as long as they want with whoever they borging well want to. Many fathers find that hard to handle for good and bad reasons. The good reason is that you want your daughter to be happy and safe; the bad reason is jealousy which can wear the acceptable face of no boy is good enough for my daughters (so nobody better get close). The only research on this subject is not direct, however. It looks at whether girls who report abuse felt their fathers were jealous of them when they had boyfriends. Not surprisingly, over 80% said they felt their fathers were jealous. But this is not a normal sample – the girls had been abused – and the research looked at what girls imagined their fathers felt.

One kind of row seems to me also exceptionally hard to deal with, and I find it curious that it is not even asked about as a question in the surveys in the 1960s and 1970s. I call these the Garbo rows in honour of Garbo's famous cry 'I want to be alone'. The conflict is about taking part in family life. Parents want the teenager to be with them while the teenager embraces being alone and spends hours locked away in their room listening to music,

watching TV, watching MTV or playing computer
games. Gunter and McAleer (1990) found that, in the
UK, the average teenager spends over 20 hours a week
in front of the television. Mark Griffiths has warned of
the addictive nature of video games.

Why do teenagers want to be alone? This is one of the
many mysteries of life psychologists have yet to answer.
But it's one thing to want to be alone à la Garbo, and
another thing to be forced to be.

Research on isolation

I know something about being a lonely teenager. When I
was 10, I used to hate coming back from school and not
finding my mother at home. She didn't work; I had no
idea where she was. I still wasn't used to London. I developed a magic obsessional ritual for dealing with my
anxiety. I'd walk round the block of flats and Bryanston
Square twice, and if I didn't take even a peep through the
living-room window – we lived on the ground floor – to
see if she was back, then she would be back after my
second walk around. It took me about 8 minutes to do
the walk. More often than not, my ritual failed. Then,
I'd then walk to Marble Arch and back. If that failed, I
went as far as Baker Street.

I had not really conquered this anxiety by the time I
was 13. And then suddenly everything changed. Just after
my 13th birthday, my father begged me to persuade my
mother to go to Israel to sell a flat they still owned there.
He'd go bankrupt if she didn't do it. Their marriage was
unhappy; my mother distrusted him. She suspected he
wanted her out of the country so he could canoodle with
secretaries. (She called them sexretaries.) My father told

me I was now grown up enough to understand that he
needed my help to make my mother see sense. Her
family had warped her.

Eventually, my mother gave in to the pressure and
flew to Israel. After the first few days, my father often
had to be away overnight. A businessman could not
ignore 'business opportunities', he explained and there
were many in Manchester, Birmingham and other far-
off cities. I wasn't a baby. He'd be back tomorrow. And,
at first, he always was.

After a few weeks, however, we had an electrical
failure – my ever-impractical father couldn't fix a
fuse though, of course, he could discourse on Benjamin
Franklin and lightning in the Old Testament. Jehovah, is
electric, kneel! Somehow he used the fuse crisis as a reason
to move out. From then on, I lived on my own in a luxury
flat in the West End. My father never explained why he
had to go but he never asked me not to tell my mother he
had gone. I missed my mother terribly and wrote frantic
letters. Once I told her he had gone, I expected her to fly
back at once. I couldn't understand why she didn't give
me a date for her return. But days passed, weeks passed
and she still hadn't closed the sale.

My father didn't abandon me, incidentally. Sometimes, he came back to spend a night in the flat. I was
always welcome at his office in Jermyn Street. Every
Friday we ate together at smart restaurants like the Tro-
cadero or the Ecu de France. He would ask what had
happened at school and give me £10 housekeeping for
the week. In the early 1960s, this was a fabulous sum.
By 10 o'clock, I was back at the flat, alone.

I was lonely and confused. As the weeks passed, I was
terrified my school would find out. I knew 13-year-olds
were not meant to live alone. I couldn't tell anyone. I am
amazed I had the sense to get my school uniform well
pressed by Mr Bell of Seymour Dry Cleaners who kept

on asking how my mother was, but then, tactfully, dropped it. (For years afterwards I hated dry cleaners.) I had to learn how to cook or I'd be condemned to a life of TV dinners. My father arranged for a cleaning lady and, later, for some months, for an au pair to live in the flat. I lusted after Monica, the Finnish au pair, but she had a boyfriend and, after 3 months, she went off to live with him.

From the age of 13 to the age of 16, I mainly lived by myself in my grand flat just off Marble Arch. I often cried myself to sleep. I kept writing to my mother and I made what I now recognise were cries for help. Once, I turned up at synagogue in rugby shorts; the rabbi didn't ask why I did such a peculiar thing. He just told me to tell my mother never to let me come to God's temple improperly dressed. At night, I sometimes roamed the West End streets. Inevitably, I was picked up by men but I was so innocent that I had no idea what they were after at first. I soon made the discovery, useful in Erikson's terms, that I wasn't gay.

One of the more comic of my crises was fear of baldness. After I washed my hair, there seemed to be so much of it in the bath. Not only had I driven my parents away but I'd soon be bald. I spent some of the £10 a week going to a hair clinic. The trichologist explained to me he had rarely seen such a dangerous case. If I didn't go in for the full treatment I would go bald in a matter of months. He ran some sort of electric comb over my scalp every week and sold me hugely expensive red goo. I have never shampooed so faithfully in my life. It worked. Thirty years later, I still have a full head of hair. Can anyone prove to me it wasn't the treatment that did it? Teenage neurotics sometimes get it right!

At school I swotted. It was partly pride, partly fear, partly having nothing much else do. I might have been left but I could do Luther, Calvin, transubstantiation, *King*

Lear and 'is history seamless?' The only thing I hated at
school was the cadet corps, but I had the priceless
advantage of being able to forge absentee notes most
Mondays. No one at the school ever asked why I was
always sick on Mondays.

I had one accident while learning to cook. A pressure
cooker lid blew off and I got burned. I took a taxi to St
George's Hospital where no one asked why a 14-year-old
boy was alone.

I did see my mother a number of times in these 3
years, usually in Israel but sometimes in Switzerland.
Somehow the deal for the house was very complicated
and the contract had never been quite signed which was
why she could not come home.

I learned about girls and eventually when I was 15 met
Judith who was 20. Her mother had died and, within 2
weeks, she had moved into the flat. I wasn't lonely any
more. I now had to hide from my school the altogether
amazing fact that I was living with a woman.

I've written at length about this because it was a
turning point for me, just as Erikson's ideas suggest. It
damaged my relationship with both my parents, but especially with my mother to whom I had been very close. I
found it hard to forgive her especially as she refused to talk
about it ever. But my parents had their parents, Aileen
said wisely many years later. My father's father had spent
most of his adult life away from his home. My mother had
her own weird family dynamics. As my parents grew old
and, then, very old, I wanted to forgive them. I felt I
should forgive them. I still wanted them to explain why
they had done it, but we never really dealt with it.

I would love to be able to write that in the end there
was perfect love and true forgiveness. As I got into my
thirties I did forgive them – sort of. I realised they had
their own side to it – sort of. I would be lying if I said it
was the kind of forgiveness that healed everything. I

wouldn't wish any teenager to go through that kind of experience even though it had its positives and its pleasures. I learned things about myself, not to crack under pressure, to cope, but I also learned to put up with betrayals and pain perhaps more than I should. Ironically, I had managed the separation reasonably. I hadn't gone mad or tried to kill myself or done anything very extreme. But the fear of separation stayed. I can still see traces of that in me now. My experience did have one very positive effect. I was very determined not to repeat that part of my history with my children.

Conclusion

Being a good enough father to teenagers seems to me to require the generosity to let go slowly, while giving a child the secure knowledge that you are there to come back to. If you do it well, it cements your relationship for ever, I suspect. But it's not easy to do. Good enough fathering is about letting go but not about doing abruptly.

Things have changed a great deal since the 1960s. Though it was abnormal to be left at 13, most of my friends left home when they were 18. After they went to university, they did not expect to come back home to live. It's a strange comment on a society where children grow up faster than ever before that they tend to leave home much later than at any time in the last 50 years.

12

The dependency paradox

Will they ever leave home?

I wonder what Montaigne would have made of the conflicts between fathers and their children today. Three hundred and thirty years on, how much has changed? I don't think he would find it hard to find modern examples to parallel the sad Monluc who had never let his son know what he felt for him. I don't think he would find it hard to identify older fathers who are obsessed with property and the question of who would inherit their fortune.

But there are some important differences. Growing up in the 1960s, my generation could not leave home fast enough. We didn't want to live with our parents. The experience of my ex-wife Aileen was typical. She left the States as soon as she had finished college, partly to create some distance between her and her parents. Julia, the mother of Alex and Katy, left home at 18 and worked as a cleaner, sometimes, to put herself through nursing training at St Thomas.

Today, it is very different. I am writing this the day after a drink with two artist friends of mine. Elisabeth is in her early 50s. She was waiting for her daughter, who had spent 6 months in New Zealand, to come home. Elisabeth told me she has a wonderful relationship with her daughter, but she sounded a little nervous. Her daughter is lively; Elisabeth and her husband have become used to living on their own. How would they cope now their daughter was coming back? Their daughter is 26 years old and would probably stay at home till she sorted herself out.

In London, sorting out accommodation is expensive, especially as, for many chic young people, the idea of living outside Central Zone 1 seems to put their mental health at risk.

The outré outer suburbs

I take as a specimen Katy, Julia's daughter. After returning from a year's work experience in New York, she was very upset at having to live in Tufnell Park, which is apparently on the edge of the jungle. Did no one love her? In New York, she preferred to live in a hostel in Manhattan rather than have a room of her own somewhere less central. I have every sympathy.

Today in Britain, young people often come back to live at home even after they have been to college. The good enough parent provides decent food, decent drink, television, fully integrated music centres, personal computers, the phone and, of course, the roof over the head. Some parents charge rent; I advise against this. It gives youth the delusion they are paying their way and they may even think they have rights.

The rules of living together have changed. In the old days, Ma and Pa ruled. If you had to live at home, you lived on their terms. In the world of the Godfather, the junior Mafioso would never have dared bring back a girl for a shag because Mafia mum would have been outraged. I was able to wrong-foot my mother and have girls to stay, partly because when she returned to London she had totally lost the moral high ground having flitted off to foreign parts and her lover for 3 years.

But, today, the parent who wants to stop a son or daughter having someone back to stay the night has to be willing to have a fight.

Separate bedrooms? What are you dad? The Pope?

There is an additional social phenomenon which I describe as the mystery of the non-verbal partner. Alex often has girlfriends home, but they seem to pretend they are not really here. It seems to require *force majeure* to get them to say 'hello'. They rarely come out of his room. Please understand. I'm not opposed to any sex. I don't expect meaningful communication; I do not suppose they'll want to discuss the latest MTV show or green politics with either Julia or me. But a passing wave, two sentences (more or less of the sort that have been taught to chimps by American academics) would be nice.

The silence of the girlfriends is apparently his mother's fault and my fault:

'*You intimidate them,*' Alex explains.

'*How?*'

'*You're just intimidating.*'

So the best we can expect is an embarrassed 'hello' as Jenny or Mandy disappears into the bathroom, poor girls who are obviously frightened they are about to be subjected to the third degree and a psychometric test to see if they meet the criteria for being Alex's lover.

I suspect there are at least two reasons why some parents do not insist on 'their rights' when a child in his 20s or even 30s lives at home. One is that we, too, are confused; the second is that the dependency paradox is tempting. Letting go of your children is not easy. If they want to stay at home, you feel flattered. It proves you are a good parent as opposed to those too bad parents whose children hate them so much they have moved out. The temptation is to cling on to them and let them behave badly clinging on to you.

But the dependency paradox makes perfectly competent young adults infantile in some respects. Richardson (2001) has claimed that young people today only mature by the time they are 35 because we all grow up more slowly. The consolation is that we are only old, as our parents understood it, when we get to sixty.

Recently, I met a 27-year-old public-school hero, a crack shot, a competent graduate who is still living at home with mum and dad. Home is a dilapidated grand house in Ireland. His family can trace the line back to the royal house of Leinster. He is an adult, but being at home brings back childish ways. When I was there talking to his parents, his very civilised mother was scolding him for scoffing all the chocolate pudding – and leaving none for anyone else.

One result is tension – and the other is infantilisation. You can't be truly grown up, you can't be truly independent while you are still living in your parents' house. Partly, that is because there will be tensions – and some of those tensions involve re-enactments of the battles of childhood. But, now, there are serious territory conflicts.

It's worth setting out some familiar causes of tensions:

- Who uses the email on the computer?

- Who uses the washing machine and when. This is a major source of conflict in our house.
- The dishwasher – why do they never use the dishwasher.
- The question of food – I take the view that all food is shared and mind, when the children (aged mid-20s), bring back food wrapped separately.
- The mysterious disappearance of your shampoo, aftershave, perfume.
- The pervasive smell of pot.

But in my own humble experience, what I have found most difficult is being lectured on my many deficiencies. I am not talking here of the Tennessee Williams scene where the younger generation confronts parents about fundamental values. The lectures I am subjected to aren't about apartheid, the evils of nuclear bombs or why my sell-out generation is frying up the greenhouse effect.

Rather, the rows are about how I do not know how to live my life appropriately:

Do you realise that you are eating too much red meat, dad?

Do you ever count how much booze you consume?

I'm thinking of going back to karate, dad, Wouldn't that be a good thing for you to do? I don't mean to mention your paunch but ... your paunch. A run before breakfast wouldn't kill you.

Is it wise to invest in buy-to-let properties instead of a pension? Have you considered the property crash which wiped everyone out in 1988? [He was thirteen at the time and did not read the Estates Gazette as I remember.]

I am so worried about you dad!

It's all spoken with real love too, because my children care. I feel secure in their love. They want the best for me. And that seems to give them the right to dissect all my failings. I love them to bits, nevertheless, which means I listen. Aileen says to me wisely 'When the children criticise you, they're not always right.'

The wish for the replica

In the first chapter, I looked at the age-old ambivalence between fathers and sons dating back to Abraham and Isaac. Psychoanalysts suggest sometimes the conflicts are due to narcissism – the father sees himself in his son and the son will carry on 'my' essence. If my son is not only biologically like me but psychologically like me, I will be truly powerful and immortal.

Some awareness of this can be found in the writings of the radical educator A. S. Neill whose thundering against daddy as sadist I quoted earlier. In the preface to *Common Sense and the Child*, Neill also wrote of the fate of children with strong fathers. He said:

And because Daddy is possessive and likes radio and polished pianos, he takes it for granted that little Jimmy, being made in his father's image, has the same interest ... This leads to the most disas-

trous warping of the child's boy nature for the boy
is nearly always sacrificed to the grand piano ...

And the father who wants his son to follow in his footsteps has not disappeared. Sir Richard Branson announced his 15-year-old son was showing signs of being interested in the family business. The founder of easyJet, when he recently accepted an award as Entrepreneur of the Year, thanked his father because he had given him love, support, everything a son could expect – plus around £30 million to start an airline.

I use the word replica because I am a fan of the novelist Susan Howatch. In her novels about the Church of England in the 20th century, Howatch often describes psychologically fragile men whose fathers wanted to turn them into replicas. The hero of *Glamorous Powers* is Jonathan Darrow who we first meet as the abbot of an elitist abbey. Darrow's father was a schoolmaster and wanted his son to follow him into that profession. Darrow resisted for years though, in the end, he does turn out to be a gifted teacher himself. Later Jonathan has children himself, before becoming a monk, wants his son to be like him; Jonathan hates the fact that the boy has no psychic gifts, no spiritual leanings. Martin turns out to be a famous actor, gay and a drunk. Darrow is only content when his second son turns out also to have psychic gifts and is, in some sense, a replica of his old man.

I experienced these pressures myself. My father was deeply disappointed when I did not become a lawyer like him. It didn't occur to him or my mother that after leaving me, I would resist their wishes. I left school at 16 to become an actor. But my father was supportive and smart. For months, he came down to Minehead in the West Country nearly every week to see me play in seaside rep. I was the police sergeant in *Getaway with*

Murder, a very daft whodunit, the 10-year-old wisecrack-
ing New York kid in *Critic's Choice* and a village idiot in
an unspeakable play about sheep stealing in Wales.

My father suddenly became very sensitive when I was
in rep. In my less charitable moods, I think it was due to
his guilt about having left me, but he had been going to the
theatre all his adult life. He saw that I would never be a
first-rate actor. I suspect my village idiot, police sergeant
and 10-year-old were rather similar. But my father also
sensed that if he let me be, I had a better chance of being
realistic. I'd accept I'd never be a second Laurence
Olivier.

If my father had not been wise, I suspect I would have
struggled on for years trying to be an actor. If only to
prove my father wrong. As it was, after 2 years of failing
auditions and the occasional crummy part, I gave up
acting. My father couldn't contain his joy. I went to
Oxford. Often our relationship was marred – he and my
mother had a bitter divorce – but I always loved and
respected him for his good sense about giving up trying
to make me some kind of replica of him.

In the end, I became a psychologist, writer and director and, ironically, I never acted again till last year when
my son insisted on casting me in his first film. Then, I was
back playing a policeman again, as I had when I first set
foot on stage. I was, of course, flattered. It is all too human
to want your children to be like you, all too human and all
too stupid.

When I outlined what this book would be about, I did
not expect it to be so personal. I have found writing about
the father–child relationship made me think, and made me
remember, much about my father, my mother and about
my children. Maybe it was naive of me to think it
wouldn't. Being a father is not a subject one can be
simply objective about, though I think I have covered
all the relevant research currently available. I hope

readers will have found the text amusing, moving and helpful. I do not claim to have been a good father I have tried to be a good enough father. But I have certainly learned that the hopes, fears, joys, irritations, angers, moments of love, love given, love got, that happen between a father and his children are the very stuff of life. I thank my children for that.

Get fathering!

References

Astrachan, A. (1985) *How Men Feel Feel*, Anchor Books.

Apter, M. (1992) *The Dangerous Edge; the Psychology of Excitement*, Free Press.

Bartrip, J., Morton, J. and de Schonen, S. (2001) 'Infants' responses to mothers face', *Brit. J. Developmental Psychology*, 219–232.

Bartsch, K. and Wellman, H. (1995) *Children Talk About the Mind*, Oxford University Press.

Baumrind, D. (1988) *Rearing Competent Children*, Jossey Bass.

Benton, D. and Roberts, G. (1988) 'Effects of vitamin and mineral supplementation on intelligence of a sample of schoolchildren', *Lancet*, **1**, 140–144.

Bivens, J. and Berk, L. A. (1990) 'A longitudinal study of development in elementary school of child private speech', *Merrill Palmer Quarterly*, **36**, 443–463.

Blendis, J. (1988) 'Paternal involvement in child care', PhD dissertation, University of London.

Bowlby, J. (1981) *Attachment and Loss*, Penguin.

Burgoyne, J. (1987) *Divorce Matters*, Penguin.

Carlsmith, L. (1964) 'Effects of early father loss on scholastic aptitude', *Harvard Educational Review*, **34**, 3–21.

Ceci, S., Ornstein, P. and Loftus, E. (1998) 'Adult recollections of childhood abuse', *Psychology, Public Policy and Law*, 1025–1051.

Ceci, S., Bruck, M. (1999) 'The suggestibility of children', *Annual Review of Psychology*, 419–439.

Chomsky, N. (1957) *Syntactic Structures*, Mouton.

Chomsky, N. (1986) *Knowledge of Language*, Praeger.

Cohen, D. (1993) *The Development of Play*, Routledge.

Cohen, D. (1977) *Psychologists on Psychology*, Routledge.

Cohen, D. (1995) *Psychologists on Psychology*, 2nd edition, Routledge.

Cohen, D. (1999) 'Toy story', *New Scientist*, 30 October 1999.

Corby, B. (ed.) (2000) *Child Abuse*, Open University Press.

Coleman, J. (1999) *The Nature of Adolescence*, Routledge.

Crick, M. (1995) *Stranger than Fiction*, Hodder and Stoughton.

Curry, N. E. and Arnaud, S. (1984) 'Play in preschool settings', in T. Yawkey and A. Pellegrine (eds) *Child's Play Developmental and Applied*, Erlbaum.

Dawkins, R. (1989) *The Selfish Gene*, Oxford University Press.

Dreikurs, R. (1970) *Happy Parents*, Souvenir.

Dunn, J. and Cutting, A. (1999) 'Theory of mind, emotional understanding, language and family background', *Child Development*, **70**, 853–865.

Elliott, L. (1995) *Compulsive Murders*, McClelland and Stewart.

Erikson, E. (2000) *The Erik Erikson Reader*, W. W. Norton.

Ernst, M., Moolcha, E. T. and Robinson, M. (2001) 'Behavioral and neural consequences of prenatal exposure to nicotine', *J. Amer. Acad. Child Adolescent Psychiatry*, **40**, 630–647.

Eysenck, H. J. (1979) *The Structure and Measurement of Intelligence*, Springer Verlag.

Eysenck, H. J. (1995) *Genius, the Natural History of Creativity*, Cambridge University Press.

Flavell, J. H. (1962) *The Developmental Psychology of Jean Piaget*, Van Nostrand.

Flavell, J. H. (1992) 'Cognitive development, past, present and future', *Developmental Psychology*, **28**, 998–1004.

Flavell, J. H. and Wellman, H. M, (1997) 'Metamemory', in R. V. Kail and J. W. Hagen (eds) *Perspectives on the Development of Memory and Cognition*, Erlbaum. .

Flavell, J. H., Greene, F. and Flavell, E. R. (1998) 'The mind has a mind of its own', *Child Development*, **13**, 127–138.

Freud, S. (1930) *Totem and Taboo*, Hogarth Press.

Gardner, H. (1992) *Multiple Intelligences*, Basic Books.

Gerhardstein, P., Adler, S. A. and Rovee Collier, C. (2000) 'A dissociation in infants memory for stimulus size', *Developmental Psychobiology*, **36**, 123–135.

Gibbens, J. (1950) *The Care of the Young Baby*, Churchill.

Gorell Barnes, G. (1998) *Growing Up in Stepfamilies*, Clarendon Press.

Grossmith, G. (1898) *Diary of a Nobody*, now available in Dent Classics.

Gunter, B. and McAleer, S. (1990) *Children and Television, the One Eyed Monster*, Routledge.

Joseph, R. M. and Tager Flusberg, H. (1999) 'Preschool children's understanding of desire and the constraints of intentional action', *Brit. J. Development Psychology*, **17**, 221–243.

Harvey, A. (1980) 'The parent Infant relationship', *J. Roy. Soc. Medicine*, **73**, 339–352.

Hepper, P. (1991) 'Fetal learning', *Irish J. Psychology*, **12**, 95–107.

Herbert, M. (1986) *Living with Teenagers*, Blackwell.

Hill, M. (1986) *Sharing Childcare in Early Parenthood*, Routledge.

Hine, T. (1999) *The Rise and Fall of the American Teenager*, Avon.

Howatch, S. (1990) *Glamorous Powers*, Harper Collins.

Hudson, L. (1966) *Contrary Imaginations*, Penguin.

Hughes, M. (1975) 'Egocentrism in young children', unpublished PhD dissertation, Edinburgh University.

Humphries, S. and Gordon, P. (1990) *A Man's World*, BBC Books.

Kahn, H. and Cooper, C. (1993) *Stress in the Dealing Room*, Routledge.

Kail, R. and Salthouse, T. (1994) 'Processing speed as a mental capacity', *Acta Psychologica*, 199–225.

Kavanaugh, R. D. and Harris, P. L. (1999) 'Pretense and counterfactual thoughts in young children', in L. Balter (ed.) *Child Psychology*, Psychology Press.

Kilpatrick, R. and Trew, K. (1985) 'Life styles and psychological well being among unemployed men in Northern Ireland', *J. Occupational Psychology*, **58**, 207–216.

Kim Dae Jung (1996) *Prison Writings*, University of California Press.

Kline, P. (1972) *Fact and Fantasy in Freudian Theory*, Methuen.

Knijn, T. and Mulder, A. C. (1987) *Unravelling Fatherhood*, Foris Publishers.

Kohlberg, L. (1984) *The Psychology of Moral Development*, Harper and Row.

Laing, R. D. (1967) *Knots*, Penguin.

Lessing, E., Zagorin, S. W. and Nelson, D. D. (1970) 'WISC subtest and IQ correlates of father absence', *J. Genetic Psychology*, **67**, 181–195.

Lewis, C. (1986) *The Role of Fathers in the Human Family*, Open University Press.

Lewis, C. (2001) *What Good Are Dads?*, Rowntree Trust.

Lummis, T. (1982) 'The historical dimension of fatherhood', in L. McKee and M. O'Brien (eds) Tavistock.

Lynn, R. (1997) 'Geographical variation in intelligence', in H. Nyborg (ed.) *The Scientific Study of Human Nature*, Erlbaum.

McGarrigle, J. and Donaldson, M. (1975) 'Conservation accidents', *Cognition*, 341–350.

Mackintosh, N. J. (1999) *IQ and Human Intelligence*, Oxford University Press.

McGraw, M. (1945) *The Neuromuscular Maturation of the Human Infant*, Lippincott, reissued 1988.

Masson, J. (1999) *The Emperor's Embrace*, Vintage.

Meltzoff, A. N. and Moore, M. K. (1983) 'Newborn infants imitate adult facial gestures', *Child Development*, **54**(3), 702–709.

Merrill, E. (1930) *Common Sense and The Child*, with a preface by A. S. Neill, Jarrolds.

Mikes, G. (1946) *How to Be an Alien*, Deutsch.

Miles, R. (1994) *The Children We Deserve*, Harper Collins.

Montaigne, M. (*ca*. 1580) *Essays* (now available in Penguin Classics).

Moore, A. (cited in Pollock, 1984).

Mortimore, J. (1970) *A Voyage Round My Father*, Penguin.

Nelson, K. (1989) *Narratives from the Crib*, Harvard University Press.

O'Brien, S. (1986) *The Negative Scream*, Routledge.

Ornstein, R. (1998) *Multimind*, Methuen.

Orbach, S. (1998) *Fat is a Feminist Issue*, Arrow.

Orwell, G. (1938) *Coming Up for Air*, Gollancz (now available in Penguin Classics).

Palermo, G. and Ross, L. G. (1999) 'Mass murder, suicide and moral development', *International Journal of Offender Therapy and Comparative Criminology*, **43**, 8–20.

Palladino, G. (1994) *Teenagers – an American History*, Harper Collins.

Piaget, J. (1950) *The Psychology of Intelligence*, Routledge and Kegan Paul.

Piaget, J. (1952) *Play Dreams and Imitation in Childhood*, Routledge and Kegan Paul.

Plath, S. (1985) *Collected Poems*, Harper Collins.

Pollock, L. (1984) *Forgotten Children*, Cambridge University Press.

Radin, N. and Wills, E. (1999) 'The effect of father participation in child rearing: 20 year follow up', *Am. J. Orthopsychiatry*, **69**, 328–336.

Reissland, N. (1988) Neonatal imitation in the hours of life; observations from rural Nepal', *Developmental Psychology*, **24**, 464–46.

Rogers, C. (1939) *The Clinical Treatment of the Problem Child*, Houghton Mifflin.

Rovee Collier, C. (1996) 'Measuring infant memory: A critical commentary', *Developmental Review*, **16**, 301–310.

Rovee Collier, C. (1997) 'Disassociations in infant memory', *Psychological Review*, **104**, 467–498.

Salinger, J. D. (1951) *The Catcher in the Rye* (now available in Penguin Classics).

Salthouse, T. (1998) 'Pressing issues in cognitive ageing', in N. Schwarz (ed.) *Cognition, Ageing and Self*, Erlbaum.

Schmidt, L. and Fox, N. (1998) 'Fear potentiated startle response in temperamentally different infants', *Developmental Psychobiology*, **32**, 113–121.

Shelley, D. and Cohen, D. (1986) *Testing Psychological Tests*, Croom Helm.

Skinner, B. (1948) *Walden Two*, Macmillan.

Skinner, B. (1952) *Human Behaviour*, Macmillan.

Singh, D. and Newburn, M. (2000) *Becoming a Father*, National Childbirth Trust.

Sully, J. (1912) *Studies of Childhood*, Longmans.

Thomas, D. (1990) *Collected Poems*, Penguin.

Tinbergen, E. A. and Tinbergen, N. (1972) *Early Childhood Autism*, Verlag Paul Parley.

Valentine, E. W. (1942) *The Normal Child*, Penguin.

Watson, J. B. (1914) *Psychology from the Standpoint of the Behaviorist*, Lippincott.

Watson, J. B. and Rayner, R. (1929) *The Psychological Care of the Infant and Child*, Lippincott.

Wells, G. (1981) *Learning through Interaction*, Cambridge University Press.

Wilson, M. and Daly, M. (2001) 'The evolution of couple conflict', in A. Booth and C. Croucher (eds), Erlbaum.

Winnicott, D. W. (1971) *The Child, the Family and the Outside World*, Penguin.

Zahn Wexler, C., Radke Yarrow, M. and King, R. A. (1979) 'Child rearing and children's prosocial intention towards victims of distress', *Child Development*, **50**, 319–330.

Useful addresses

Some UK organisations have direct helplines.

Aspergers, Aspen P.O. Box 351268, Jacksonville, FL 32235, phone 1-866-4-ASPRGR. Also, in the UK, National Autistic Society, see below.

Barnardos, Tanners Lane, Barkingside, London IG6 1QG, phone 0208 550 8822.

Children's Society, Margery Street, London WC1X 0JL, phone 0207 841 4436.

Childline, helpline 0800 1111.

Families Need Fathers, 134 Curtain Road, London EC2A, phone 0207 613 5060.

Gingerbread, 7 Sovereign Close, Sovereign Court, London E1W 3HW, helpline 0800 018 4318.

MIND, Granta House 15–19 the Broadway, Stratford, London E15 4BQ, phone 0208 519 2122.

National Autistic Society, 393 City Road, London EC1, phone 0207 903 3563.

National Society for Deaf Children, 15 Dufferin Street, London EC1 8UR, phone 0207 250 0123.

National Society for the Prevention of Cruelty to Children (NSPCC), 42 Curtain Road, London EC2 A3N, helpline 0808 800 5000, parentline 0800 800 2222.

National Society for the Protection of the Child, helpline 0808 800 5000 for child protection.

Royal National Institution for the Blind, Great Portland Street, London W1, helpline 0845 788 9999.

Young Minds (excellent mental health resource), 102–108 Clerkenwell Road, London EC1M 5SA, phone 0207 336 8445.

Index